Non Fic

Charles, The Man & The Prince

This revised edition is updated to the day of the royal wedding. While retaining all the best features of the original edition, it has been extended to include the story of the new Princess of Wales, of her ancestry, upbringing and home life. Additionally it tells of how Prince Charles wooed and won her, and a colourfully descriptive account of the wedding day. A book for everyone who wishes to know more about the royal life than can be glimpsed on television.

CHARLES
The Man & The Prince
by
Graham & Heather Fisher

MAGNA PRINT BOOKS
Long Preston, North Yorkshire,
England.

British Library Cataloguing in Publication Data

Fisher, Graham
    Charles: the man and the prince.—
    Large print ed
    1. Charles, *Prince of Wales*   2. Great Britain—
    Princes and princesses—Biography
    I. Title   II. Fisher, Heather
    941.085′092′4   DA591.A33

    ISBN 0-86009-563-0

First Published in Great Britain by Robert Hale 1977. Revised 1981.

Copyright © 1977 & 1981 by Graham & Heather Fisher

Published in Large Print 1984 by arrangement with Robert Hale Ltd London and the Copyright holders.

Photoset in Great Britain by
Dermar Phototypesetting Co., Long Preston, North Yorkshire.

Printed and bound in Great Britain by
Redwood Burn Limited, Trowbridge.

CONTENTS

Preface 11
Curriculum Vitae 15
1 Man and Wife 19
2 Child 58
3 Schoolboy 91
4 Student 130
5 Entertainer 158
6 Apprentice 180
7 Sportsman 217
8 Flyer 237
9 Sailor 246
10 Bachelor 264
11 Suitor 296
12 Prince and Princess 308
Appendices
I Appointments, Presidences, Patronages Held by Prince Charles 389
II Education 395
III Prince of Wales 397
IV Overseas Tours and Visits 399
V Flying and Naval Career 405
VI Witty Ditty 409

PICTURE CREDITS

PREFACE

The material on which this book is based is drawn from three sources.

The first is Prince Charles himself. No other member of the Royal Family, surely, has ever talked so fully and so frankly. Over the past few years there has been interview after interview; on radio and television, in newspapers and magazines. So it is possible to assess him, as both prince and man, on the basis of his own statements and admissions. Of course, as he has said himself, what he thinks today he may not necessarily think tomorrow. Opinions change with the years. But facts remain facts.

The second source is our own research over the years. No man sees himself exactly as others see him, so we have drawn also upon facts and opinions obtained from people who have known him at various stages of his life; who have been with him at various times and places.

The third source is what others have written about him. Over the years acres of paper and hogsheads of printing ink have been devoted to chronicling every detail of his life. In drawing on this third source, we have done our best to sort the wheat from the chaff. Some of what has been written about him has been inaccurate, some has been exaggerated and some has been genuflecting in the extreme...like the forecast that he would make a 'jolly good king'.

He was seven when that was written, which would seem to make it a rather premature judgement. It is perhaps more accurate to say that if he had not changed a great deal between then and now he would have made—to use the same schoolboy vernacular—'a jolly poor king'.

But he has changed, as all of us do with the years. Schooldays, university, life in the navy, marriage...all these things have moulded and developed his character. Today most people would happily go along with the view that some time in the future he will make a 'a jolly good king'.

And when that day comes, he will have by his side a wife the whole world has immediately taken to its heart. As Princess of Wales and sometime Queen, we predict with confidence, his young bride will prove herself a consort cast in much the same mould as the Queen Mother... slightly shyer perhaps, but as loving and supportive of her husband, as dutiful and devoted to Britain and the Commonwealth.

Keston Park
Kent.

G. and H.F.

CURRICULUM VITAE

Name:	Charles Philip Arthur George Mountbatten-Windsor
Style and Titles:	His Royal Highness The Prince of Wales and Earl of Chester, Duke of Cornwall and Duke of Rothesay, Earl of Carrick and Baron Renfrew, Lord of the Isles and Great Steward of Scotland, KG (1958), KT (1977), GCB (1975)
Height:	5feet 11 inches
Eyes:	Blue
Hair:	Brown
Born:	Buckingham Palace, London, 14th November 1948
Mother:	Queen Elizabeth II
Father:	Prince Philip, Duke of Edinburgh

Married:	St Paul's Cathedral, 29th July 1981, to Lady Diana Frances Spencer, youngest daughter (born 1st July 1961) of Earl Spencer of Althorp, Northamptonshire, and the Honourable Mrs Frances Shand-Kydd
Residence:	Highgrove, near Tetbury, Gloucestershire

FOR OUR FRIENDS
ON KESTON PARK AND
FARNBOROUGH PARK

1 Man and Wife

Some time before Lady Diana Spencer came into his life, Prince Charles was philosophizing on the subject of marriage.

'Whatever your place in life,' he said, 'when you marry you are forming a partnership you hope will last for fifty years. So I would want to marry someone whose interests I could share.'

'A woman not only marries a man; she marries into a way of life—a job. She's got to have some knowledge of it, some sense of it; otherwise she wouldn't have a clue about whether she is going to like it.'

The tall, blue-eyed blonde who became the first Princess of Wales for more than seventy years when she and Charles were married in St Paul's Cathedral on 29th July 1981, might have been specially packaged in accordance with his philosophical outlook; born and bred to dovetail neatly into both his way of life and his role as a professional prince. On a personal level, the two of them have many interests in common—music, ballet, dancing, skiing, a love of country life. 'Totally compatible', her sister, Lady Sarah McCorquodale, terms them. Both, as far as one can judge, are sincere and sensitive, and both are equipped with an abounding sense of humour. More than anything, a sense of humour is essential to survive in the endless round of tree plantings, plaque unveilings, hospital openings, factory inspections, foundation stone layings, speech making and hand shaking which will be their lot throughout married life. As Charles has also said: 'The most important thing a person in my position can have is a sense of humour...being able to laugh at oneself.'

In accepting Charles' proposal of marriage, Diana—or Princess Charles, as Buckingham Palace tells us we must now call her—also had 'some knowledge' of what she was letting herself in for; 'some sense' of the new and very different way of life upon which she would be embarking. As Princess of Wales, and later Queen, her married life will be lived in a goldfish bowl —peered at, examined, inspected from every conceivable angle. Everything she does and says, her clothes, her appearance, behaviour, demeanour, health, will all be the subject of endless reportage, speculation, gossip, approval, criticism. Cameras will be trained on her all the days of her life. Gone for ever is the informal privacy she knew before the newspapers homed in on her as 'the new girl in Charles' life'.

Charles, of course, has been forced to endure the glare of the public spotlight from the moment he was born. She has not, but the indications are that she will make out all right. Certainly she faces the future with optimism. 'With Prince Charles beside me', she says, 'it can't go wrong.' Certainly too she has a lot going for her—poise, charm, dignity, an air of innocence, of vulnerability almost, which won her a deal of public sympathy and approval even before their betrothal was announced.

And if she knew nothing of public life until the betrothal, she has a wealth of background to stand her in good stead. On one side of her family tree, she is descended several times over from that earlier

Charles, the "merry monarch" of many mistresses. She and today's Charles are in fact related, cousins so distant as to afford no genetic problems.

On the other side of her heritage, she comes down from the illustrious Churchill family. Her family have been courtiers for generations. A sixteenth-century ancestor, John Spencer, was knighted by Henry VIII. A later Spencer, 2nd Earl of Sunderland, was confidant to no fewer than three monarchs, Charles II, James II and William III. The 2nd Earl Spencer was sufficiently close to George III and Queen Charlotte for them to be godparents to his daughter. The 4th Earl held the office of Lord Chamberlain. The 5th Earl was Groom of the Stole to Queen Victoria's husband, the Prince Consort, and later to the Prince of Wales who became King Edward VII.

Coming to the present day, the new Princess's father numbered Queen Mary and the Duke of Windsor among his godparents. In early manhood he served as equerry to the late King George VI and then to the Queen for the first two years of her reign. The Queen, Prince Philip and the Queen Mother were among the wedding guests at his first marriage in Westminster Abbey in 1954. Her maternal grandmother, Lady Fermoy, has been a close friend to Charles' grandmother, as well as her lady-in-waiting, for many years. Her maternal grandfather, the 4th Baron Fermoy, was equally a close friend of Charles' dead grandfather. So close, indeed, that he was one of the last people to see the King alive. The two of them had been out rough shooting at Sandringham. 'Best day's sport I've had in a long time,' the King said to him as he unlaced his boots at the end of the day. 'We'll go again on Thursday.' Sadly, the King did not live to keep that date with his old friend. That same night he died in his sleep.

In a sense, Prince Charles has married not only a family friend, but the girl next door. Diana Spencer was born, like her mother before her, at Sandringham, in Park House, within easy walking distance of the "Big House" which has been the Norfolk home of the Royal Family since Edward VII was a young Prince of Wales.

She was born on 1st July 1961. With two daughters already, Sarah and Jane, her parents may perhaps have been hoping for a boy to take the place of the baby son who, tragically, had died within a few hours of birth the previous year. However, the baby turned out to be another girl—birthweight 7 pounds 12 ounces—and her parents were to wait another three years before finally adding a son, Charles, to their brood.

Diana's birth, on a scorching hot summer's day, meant that her mother had to forgo the York Minster wedding of the Duke and Duchess of Kent at which the eldest daughter, Sarah, was a bridesmaid. The christening of the third daughter—Diana Frances—was in the parish church in Sandringham Park. Ironically, the future Princess of Wales was the only Spencer of her generation not to number a royal sponsor among her godparents. Sister Sarah had the Queen Mother as a godmother, Jane has the Duke of Kent as godfather and the Queen herself was to be among those who sponsored young Charles.

Early childhood years were spent largely amidst the rural surroundings of Sandringham with the Royal Family as next-door neighbours at Christmas and other times. Diana and Prince Charles must have seen each other when the two families attended the parish church on Sunday mornings, but they have no recollection of it all these years later. That they did not know each other in childhood is understandable. Charles, nearly thirteen years her senior, was already a schoolboy at Cheam when she was born. While he was often at Sandringham during the holidays, sometimes with his parents and sometimes with his grandmother, the difference in their ages was too great in those early years—by the time she was ten he was already a cadet at Dartmouth—for him to have taken any notice of her or her of him. It was his younger brothers, Andrew in particular, with whom she played from time to time in childhood.

Indeed, it is said that there was sometimes a youthful telephone call to Park House. 'May we come over and swim in your pool, please?' The Spencer children had their own heated pool at Park House and the Royals had no pool.

Her education was in keeping with the family's station in life. There was a governess first, then a private school in nearby King's Lynn—she was 'a bright, lively little girl', the headmistress remembers—then a preparatory school elsewhere in Norfolk before West Heath, an exclusive boarding school for girls in Kent. Academically, she was 'about average'. She played tennis and lacrosse, kept guinea pigs, twice winning prizes with them at the Sandringham fur and feather show. She was eight when her parents divorced; fourteen when her father inherited the title of Earl Spencer—he was previously Viscount Althorp—and they moved from Park House to the family estate at Althorp in Northamptonshire. At sixteen, the age at which she met Charles for the first time, she was chief bridesmaid when her sister Jane married Robert Fellowes, who is now the Queen's assistant private secretary.

There was a short spell at a finishing school in Switzerland, where she learned to ski, after which she worked in London, though there was no need for her to have done so, as a nanny, a cook and a kindergarten teacher. Her father bought her a flat which she shared with three other girls who also shared the rent, the housework

26

and, in due course, the secret of her engagement to Prince Charles.

We have his word for it that the new Princess of Wales is 'amusing, great fun, full of life'. He himself is certainly all those things. The speech he gave when, like his father before him, he was made an honorary member of the Grand Order of Water Rats was one of which Bob Hope need not have been ashamed.

'I always get a bit anxious when I hear that I am following in my father's footsteps. I seem to spend my life doing that.

'Fortunately we wear the same size shoes.

'I also followed him to his tailor, which can be a somewhat harassing experience.

'It's one of the reasons we both walk with our hands behind our backs.

'I don't know whether you realise how horrifying it is for an inexperienced person like myself to follow such a dazzling array of comedians. It is very, very difficult indeed and I have been worrying about it constantly for the last—well, for a week at least.

'I was particularly worried about following King Rat because I saw in a brochure which was sent me the other day, warning me what to expect when I got here, that he produced a "solid support act" in his professional existence. Somehow I conjured up the most fearful images of what a "solid support act" might be.

'It sounds rather like a travelling underwear salesman.'

Pause for laughter.

'The prospect of finding ways of amusing and entertaining such a vast and hideously professional gallery of show-business personalities has led me for the first time in my life to seek the services of a ghost-writer.

'Such ethereal creatures are hard to locate, but with the help of the Metropolitan Police ghost squad and Jimmy Edwards' agent—who offered to be my agent, I may tell you (more laughter)— some of you must know him (yet more laughter)—a suitably spectral author was tracked down in one of the more salubrious quarters of London. Upon investigation, his terms seemed surprisingly reasonable—one hair from the head of each of my many girl-friends, a cup of Metropolitan Police tea, the tail of a

Grand Water Rat and a pair of my pyjamas now on loan to *Woman's Own.*'*

There was, of course, no ghost-writer, ethereal or otherwise. He—like his witch's-brew fee of feminine hair, police tea, rat's tail and princely pyjamas—was a figment of Charles' sometimes zany imagination. Charles wrote the speech himself.

In the conversational exchange before and after lunch he also showed himself to be quick on the draw when it comes to ad-libbing. For instance, he found that the menu was written in Welsh with not-too-serious English translations, the first course being interpreted as *Cold Broth of Corgi.*

'Ah, I thought there was one fewer around when I came down to breakfast this morning,' he quipped.

Even the Queen, not normally noted for the lightness of her speeches, might be expected to inject a mild joke or two into a lunch gathering of so many comedians.

*INTERVIEWED ON BEHALF OF THE MAGAZINE, CHARLES HAD BEEN ASKED WHETHER OR NOT HE WORE PYJAMAS IN BED. HE DECLINED TO ANSWER— A RARE THING WITH HIM.

But with Charles it was hardly more than par for the course. Back in his undergraduate days he had already learned the trick of sweetening the pill with a gag or two.

The Cambridge Union was debating the old Man *v.* Machine chestnut in a new-style guise: whether the technological advance of mankind threatens the individuality of man.

'I hear that in America,' said Charles in his speech, 'they spray so much insecticide around that even cannibals have begun to complain that Americans taste of DDT.'

He amused—and calmed—a somewhat excitable Industry and Environment Conference by standing up and prefacing his speech with the intriguing observation: 'As the bishop said to the actress, this thing is bigger than both of us.'

He spoke in a similarly *risqué* vein when he turned up at the Royal Thames Yacht Club to unveil a Vasco Lazzolo sculpture of his father. His speech that day started by denying that 'I am accustomed in any way to unveiling busts' and ended with the words: 'I now complete the process of helping my father to expose himself.'

On the other hand, he was—or pretended to be—concerned that actress Susan Hampshire was revealing too much of herself when he met her after a charity show at the Theatre Royal, Windsor. Miss Hampshire was dressed for the occasion in a low-cut, backless gown. 'My father told me that if I ever met a lady in a dress like yours, I must look her straight in the eyes,' said Charles, looking her straight in the eyes. 'Otherwise someone might take a photograph of me in what might appear to be a compromising attitude.'

Then there was the theatrical luncheon he was obliged to attend in morning dress (because he was going on to a society wedding). 'I am not here to audition for the part of the butler,' he said, amid laughter.

Inevitably there are times when he repeats himself or comes close to it. The Water Rats' luncheon was not the first time he had cracked the hands-behind-our-backs gag. He also came out with it, though in slightly different form, at an annual dinner of the Master Tailors' Benevolent Association.

'I am often asked,' he said on that

occasion, 'whether it is because of some generic trait that I stand with my hands behind my back, like my father.

'The answer is that we both have the same tailor.

'He makes our sleeves so tight that we can't get our hands in front.'

The tailors' function was also the occasion for one of his perhaps sometimes rather schoolboyish practical jokes. It all started with a comment in the *Tailor & Cutter* concerning his taste in clothes. Possibly disappointed because the present-day Prince of Wales has shown no sign of developing into the leader of men's fashion that the late Duke of Windsor was in his day, the *Tailor & Cutter,* which had once praised him so lavishly and ridiculously in childhood,* now did a complete switch and accused him of adopting 'the cult of studied shabbiness'. Amused rather than irritated by this (as father Philip might have been), Charles turned up at the dinner wearing a tweed jacket over his evening shirt.

More and more over the years, in both

*CHAPTER 2

public and private, the young man who will one day be King Charles III has shown himself to have a tremendous sense of humour. In private it has perhaps always been there. As a child, he was frequently playing practical jokes. The day before the late President Eisenhower was expected, for instance, he bounced in on his parents wearing a home-made 'I like Ike' badge which a friendly footman had devised for him. But in public his sense of humour was hidden earlier on behind the acute shyness which is a family trait handed down from his mother and maternal grandfather and a self-conscious awareness of his unique position as the Queen's eldest son. Only gradually, as he has conquered his shyness and overcome his self-consciousness, has the private man shown through the public prince.

His quips and jokes are fast becoming the stuff of royal legend. There is, for instance, the story of how during his spell at Timbertop he went round telling everyone that one of the things he was being taught there was the way to catch kangaroos. The method, apparently, was to creep up on them from behind, grab them by the tail and then flip them smartly over on to their backs.

Some people believed him!

Then there was the time, at Trinity College, when he encountered a dust-covered senior tutor, Denis Marrian, emerging from the wine cellar in the college courtyard.

Commented Charles, slyly: 'I've always wondered where the senior tutor lived.'

There was another occasion, underground at Welbeck colliery, chatting with a miner. The poor chap had just had the misfortune to lose his set of false teeth. They had dropped out of his mouth, he told Charles, and been whipped away on the conveyor belt before he could grab them back.

'Ah,' observed Charles, 'I thought I passed a grin coming in.'

In Brisbane he stood in the wings with comedian Des O'Connor to watch the second half of Australia's first-ever Royal Variety Show. Watching, the two of them began to gag back and forth in their own private double act. 'We ought to go on stage for the benefit of the audience,' O'Connor quipped at one point.

'Yes, but what about the billing?' Charles gagged back.

His humour is sometimes subtle, sometimes zany, sometimes sexy, sometimes basic...as with a joke he told during a television interview with Cliff Michelmore and Brian Connell.

'When I went to Llanelli not long ago the mayor said, "Can you say Llanelli?" and I said, "Llanelli," and he wiped the saliva out of his eye and said, "Well done".'

Another example. He was in the Canadian Arctic, swaddled in caribou fur against the below-freezing cold. 'I hope we don't meet a polar bear,' he joked. 'He might think I'm in season.'

But royal jokes, as Prince Philip has occasionally found out to his cost, can sometimes misfire, Charles was to learn the same lesson. On that same trip to Canada, prior to setting off for the frozen north, he told a laughing audience in Ottawa: 'I have to be very careful when I look at a female. If I look more than once, they are immediately sized up as a future spouse. I imagine I shall have to be very careful on my trip north, especially with whom I rub noses.'

As a joke, it would seem to have been harmless and amusing enough, but Canada's Eskimos apparently took exception to it and Charles subsequently apologized for 'a very bad joke, a bad cliché'.

Despite such small and occasional sideslips, a sense of humour of this order is clearly a considerable asset to someone so much in the public eye. It eases tension, turneth away wrath and makes for popularity. Charles knows this and is grateful for it. There are also, of course, times when it can be something of a liability: 'terribly dangerous', as Charles conceded in an interview with David Frost.

Those who saw the television film *Royal Family* will perhaps recall an episode in which the Queen is heard telling others of the family what happened on one occasion when she was receiving a succession of ambassadors. One of her aides bent over and whispered to her. 'The next one in is a gorilla.' Or words to that effect. Sure enough, the next ambassador to be presented was both extremely hairy and long in the arm.

'I'm sure I'd have burst out laughing,' Charles says, interrupting his mother.

There has in fact been more than one public occasion on which he has found the attendant pomp and ceremony almost too much for his sense of humour; when he has caught himself conjuring up a mental picture of the most absurd thing that could conceivably happen...like the ceremonial platform with its contingent of top brass gliding down the slipway at a ship-launching ceremony.

'They're disappearing. They're waving. All that's left on the water is a couple of flowered hats and a bowler hat.'

When his fertile imagination conjures up that sort of absurdity, it takes him all his time to keep from laughing. And it is more than he dare do to meet the eyes of whoever happens to be with him. To do so, he knows, would be to court giggling disaster. 'I have to keep a straight face and control myself.'

From where does Charles get his tremendous sense of humour? From his father, Prince Philip? Hardly. Philip has a sometimes biting wit, but that is not quite the same thing. There is nothing in the smallest degree biting or caustic about the son's jokes. From his mother, then? Surely not. The Queen's sense of fun, in the privacy of the family circle, is perhaps greater than you might imagine, but shyness and her awareness of her unique position have seldom permitted her to display it in public as Charles seems to do at any and every opportunity.

Hazarding what can, in the circumstances be only a reasoned guess, we would venture the opinion that Charles' boundless sense of humour has been inherited from his grandmother, the Queen Mother. Contrast his childhood 'I Like Ike' joke with the young Elizabeth Bowes-Lyon who once posed as a maid to show visitors round her ancestral home and, if the story can be believed, even accepted a tip for her pains. Compare his antics on stage during his student days at Cambridge with those of the teenage girl who, substituting for her mother at the organ of the castle chapel, also substituted the rip-roaring strains of *Yip-I-Addy-I-Ay* for the more sober music of Handel. Consider his polar bear joke alongside the occasion when the Queen Mother, in the days when she was Queen, was at a banquet and someone sitting near her asked the meaning of a Latin inscription on a gold goblet.

'I think,' said someone else, 'that it probably says something like "Long live the Queen".'

'Perhaps we had better get it properly translated,' interposed the Queen Mother. 'For all we know, it may say, "To hell with the Queen".'

Indeed, the jokes of grandmother and grandson sometimes contain a shared chord of similarity.

The Queen Mother, paying her annual visit to the Sandringham Women's Institute a winter or so back, found it necessary to pick her way between crates of empty beer bottles in order to enter the village hall.

'I hope no one takes a picture of us,' she joked to the Queen, who was with her, 'or people will think we have been drinking.'

Compare this with Charles' 'compromising attitude' remark to Susan Hampshire. Or his comment when he found himself standing under a sign 'Drug Store' during a royal walkabout in

London on the occasion of his parents' silver wedding anniversary. 'That's all I need. Someone to take my picture underneath that.'

Whether or not his sense of humour stems from his grandmother, there are other qualities in him, at least in the Queen Mother's view, inherited from his dead grandfather, King George VI. To the Queen Mother, he is, in so many ways, his grandfather all over again, as conscientiously dutiful, as ploddingly determined, as occasionally obstinate. If there is yet another inheritance from the same source, he keeps it successfully hidden most of the time. Yet there has been the odd occasion on which he has given vent to the famous Windsor temper.

There was the time he was preparing to take an early dip from a Sydney beach when a couple of bright boys proceeded to make fun of him. Charles, we have been told, sent them on their way with some blunt Anglo-Saxon phrasing which his grandfather could not have bettered and of which father Philip would have been proud.

His language was perhaps more restrained, though his anger was obvious, the day he captained Nassau in a polo game against Freeport. The cause of his anger was the somewhat laboured humour of the commentator. A joke that 'polo should not be confused with polio, though it can become a disease' was perhaps no worse than some of Charles' own efforts on occasion, but when there was pretended confusion over his parentage— 'Prince Charles, son of...er...now, who is it?...oh yes, Queen Elizabeth'— he clearly felt that the limit had been reached. Red in the face, though perhaps more from anger than embarrassment, he dismounted and stomped up the steps of the commentary box to inform the commentator in no uncertain terms that he was turning the affair from a polo game into 'a barn dance'.

That was in 1973 and if the Prince has lost his temper since it is not a matter of public record. It is probable that he has not and possible that he will never do so again; that, like his mother, he has now learned the knack of conveying royal displeasure with no more than an icy glare.

Mother and son are alike in so many ways—dutiful, conscientious, stubborn —that it would not be surprising if there was the occasional clash of wills. But they are linked also by a real bond of true affection. 'A marvellous person and a wonderful mother,' Charles has said of the Queen. Her own nature may not permit her to talk publicly of her son in equally affectionate terms, but the love she has for him can be clearly seen in her eyes, sometimes happy for him, sometimes worried for him, always proud of him, whenever they are together.

And on the one occasion in recent years when the situation permitted her to speak affectionately in public without any sense of embarrassment, she was quick to take advantage of the fact. It was after the Prince of Wales' investiture ceremony at Caernarvon, when the Queen presented him to the crowd outside the castle. 'My most dear son,' she called him, and clearly meant it as personally as it was said publicly.

Beneath the surface of their respective public images, the Queen's *mystique* and the Prince's jocularity, both mother and son are a shade more emotional than you might perhaps imagine. Moments of high emotion—like her coming-of-age speech in South Africa, the cheers of the crowd as she drove to her crowning in Westminster Abbey, a particular moment of welcome in Australia and another in Canada—have been known to move the Queen to tears or almost to tears. Charles was similarly moved—tears, he has said, 'almost rolled down my cheeks'—by a native feast given in his honour in New Guinea. He had been greeted by the traditional rumble of jungle drums. Suddenly the drums ceased and in their place, immediately and unexpectedly, came the singing of *God Save The Queen*.

'It was the most moving, touching thing I have ever experienced,' Charles has recalled, 'to see these people, miles from Britain, singing the National Anthem.'

A young man with the Prince's reputation for risking his neck as a helicopter pilot and steeplechaser will perhaps dislike being termed 'emotional', though his own words suggest that he is.

He can hardly object to being labelled 'human' and this he certainly is. It was the Queen Mother who once referred to him as having 'a kind heart'. All grandmothers, of course, are inclined to be a trifle biased where their grandchildren are concerned and in any event it was said a long time ago. But the years since have done nothing to disprove it.

It was surely 'a kind heart' which persuaded him, during a short private visit to Paris not long after his investiture as Prince of Wales, to call upon the Duke of Windsor, the first member of his immediate family to visit the ageing self-exiled Royal in his own home. Charles stayed for about an hour. One cannot know what the two of them talked about, of course, but it must surely have been a touching occasion for both of them, the young man of twenty-one who had been invested as Prince of Wales only months before and the ageing Duke who had undergone the same ceremony of investiture well over half a century before.

And it was surely personal humanity rather than merely because he conceived it to be his royal duty which caused him

44

to visit Margaret Liles, the young police-woman who had a foot amputated, and other victims of the Moorgate Tube disaster as they lay in hospital. Had he been seeking simply to polish the princely image, then he would surely have gone earlier, bumping accidentally on purpose into the newspaper reporters and television crews gathered for a press conference. Instead of which, he waited until the press gathering was over before going along to St Bartholomew's hospital, not even informing the police of his movements.

If Charles is more like his mother and maternal grandfather in many aspects of his character, if his sense of humour derives from the Queen Mother, then physically he is almost the spit image of his father; the same ramrod stance, the same raking walk, the same look of an athlete fresh from the shower, the same speaking voice, the same tricks of ramming one hand deep in his jacket pocket or standing with hands clasped behind his back.

It would perhaps be considered unmanly of him to refer to his father in the same sort of affectionate terms he has used in talking of his mother. But affection can be sensed just the same when he speaks of Philip as 'a moderating influence' on his life and also 'an influence of great wisdom'.

Standing hands behind back is not the only thing, consciously or otherwise, which he has copied from his father. Philip's maxims for royal success are: Stand up straight, speak out and look people straight in the eye. Whatever he was like in boyhood, Charles, these days, practises all three and the straight-in-the-eye bit in particular can be a trifle disconcerting to those meeting him for the first time.

The eyes which look people straight in the eye are blue. His hair is brown. He has the sort of out-jutting ears for which Clark Gable was famous, a face which can be broadly grinning or seriously broody according to mood and occasionally, if he needs time to think, has been seen to fall back on the family habit —the late Duke of Windsor did the same —of smoothing the back of his hair with his hand.

He has a 37-inch chest, a 31-inch waist and stands an inch under 6 feet in height. As a small boy he suffered from the chestiness which seems to run in the Royal Family. He also suffered most of the customary ailments of childhood: measles (which caused a worried head-master at Cheam to cable daily bulletins to his parents during their royal tour of Pakistan), chicken pox (which he took home from school and passed on to Anne) and tonsillitis (twice). On the second occasion the offending tonsils were whipped out and later his appendix was similarly excised. Since then a robust combination of sleeping with the dormi-tory windows open at Cheam, early-morning jogtrots and cold showers at Gordonstoun and shipboard life in the Navy would seem to have turned him into as healthy as specimen of young manhood as ever dropped his trousers and coughed for medical inspection. He does not smoke, drinks in moderation and enjoys life most when it has a touch of adventure, even danger, to it. 'If you are living dangerously, it tends to make you appreciate life much more and really want to live it to the fullest.'

Whether or not he wears pyjamas in bed may be a closely-guarded royal secret, but there are few other things we do not know about him. He has talked too freely about himself to have kept much else secret. We know that he prefers field sports to team sports (with the exception of polo), classical music to pop, collects soapstone carvings, is mad on pre-history, loathes mathematics, is a television 'natural' without being a television addict (though he enjoys programmes like *Monty Python* and *The Goodies),* has a taste for rather juvenile practical jokes and we have his mother's word for it that he likes uglies (a cross between a grapefruit and a tangerine) for breakfast.

He was asked in the course of one interview how he saw himself. The question may have caught him off-guard and in a reply which was perhaps part joke, part nervousness and part an excess of modesty he shrugged himself off as 'a twit'. Most people would agree that it was also an inaccurate personal assessment. But not, of course, that arch-opponent of monarchy, Member of Parliament William Hamilton. He labelled Charles 'a young twerp' while making a forlorn attempt to persuade Parliament to nationalize the Prince's Duchy of Cornwall estate. Charles has been given not a few other equally hurtful labels in the course of his young life. He was called 'fatty' at Cheam, 'a moron' at Gordonstoun, 'a royal borderliner' when he first went to Cambridge and 'a crank' by the mayor of a Melbourne suburb after he had criticized the condition of the local beach. More sensitive than his father—who is also more sensitive than he would admit—Charles has sometimes been hurt by such digs.

But if some people have been unkind or unfair in their references to him, others sometimes go to the other extreme. He has been termed 'a natural' so many times—a television natural, a helicopter natural, a natural pilot—that the word is in danger of becoming overworked. Writers in women's magazines are fond of referring to him in such sugar-coated terms as 'a Prince Charming' which make him squirm with embarrassment.

He has also been referred to as 'a square' and this he is in the sense that he believes firmly in such old-fashioned values as honesty, decency and the unity of family life. He is perhaps 'a square' in other ways too.

'I dare say,' he told the Society of Magazine Editors a year or so back, 'that I could improve my image in some circles by growing my hair to a more fashionable length, being seen in the Playboy Club at frequent intervals and squeezing myself into excruciatingly tight clothes.' But he had no intention, he added, of adopting any such course of action.

'I am not a rebel by temperament,' he said on another occasion around the same time. 'I don't get a kick out of not doing what is expected of me or doing what is not expected of me.'

If his tendency to live dangerously at times would seem to echo the Gordonstoun school motto *Plus est en vous* (There is more in you), there is another motto which equally governs the rest of his life-style. It is the traditional motto of the Prince of Wales: *Ich Dien* (I Serve).

'I think *I Serve* is a marvellous motto,' Charles has said, 'and I think it is the basis of one's job: to serve other people. If you have a sense of duty—and I like to think I have—then service is something that you give yourself to people, particularly if they want you and sometimes if they don't.'

In an age when many other people are finding their family ties gradually disintegrating, it is an interesting and heartening anomaly that the present bunch of Royals, as a family, should be closer knit than perhaps any previous royal generation. 'I think of my family as very special people,' Charles has said. 'We happen to be a very close-knit family.'

Between Charles and his mother, as indeed between her and her father when he was on the throne, there exists not a scrap of the fear, suspicion, envy and rancour which divided Monarch from Heir over so many royal generations. The matriarchal Queen Victoria never really liked or completely trusted the Prince of Wales who was finally to succeed her as Edward VII and right up

51

to her death at the ripe old age of eighty-one would not permit him to play his full and proper part in the royal scheme of things.* Edward VII, in turn, brought up his Heir to be in awe of him and that Heir, George V, did the same with his. Which perhaps accounts, in part at least, for the fact that the Duke of Windsor, when his time came, kicked over the royal traces.

Far from Charles being in awe of his mother, far from her distrusting him, there has existed between them always a close and loving relationship. Far from not letting Charles play his full part in royal affairs, his mother has consistently extended the boundaries of his public role, training him by example towards the day when he will take over from her. Philip too has played his part in his son's coaching towards future monarchy and if, earlier on, he made the mistake of trying to mould Charles too closely to his

*ANYONE WHO WOULD LIKE TO KNOW MORE ABOUT THE STRAINED RELATIONSHIP BETWEEN QUEEN VICTORIA AND HER ELDEST SON CAN FIND IT IN OUR BOOK *BERTIE AND ALIX*.

own more thrusting image, the reasons are understandable and it would seem that no harm has been done.

For too long Charles was perhaps inclined to live in the shadow of his father, for a small boy a somewhat awe-inspiring figure with a reputation for rugged masculinity and brilliant sportsmanship. There was perhaps at that time, on the son's side, a sense of rivalry with his father or, at very least, a necessity to emulate him, to be the sort of boy the father had been in his day. Following in father's more athletic footsteps at Cheam and Gordonstoun can hardly have helped and it was not until later, at Timbertop and Trinity, with no Philip to live up to, that Charles began to find himself and realize his true potential.

With sister Anne, as with Andrew and Edward, the young ones of the family, he has an affectionate brotherly relationship. In fact, he gets on better with Anne these days than he did when they were children together and her teasing, more extrovert personality largely overshadowed and dominated his shyer, quieter nature. He thinks that the media are sometimes unfair to his sister and instances what happened when her horse fell down during an eventing championship in Moscow. 'It is easy to become irritable and feel that it is only when you fall off that the press are interested; that it is only when you are upside down or halfway up a tree that photographs appear in the papers or on television.'

Charles himself contrives to use the media for his own ends as no other member of the Royal Family has ever done. In interview after interview, on radio and television, in newspapers and magazines, he has talked freely, frankly and at length on almost every royal topic under the sun, from his schooldays at Gordonstoun to the possibility that the Queen might abdicate (he doesn't like the idea), from his relationship with his parents to the details of his courtship.

Indeed, far from seeking to escape his inquisitors, there have been times when he has sought to become yet more involved. When the BBC made a television film of his flying and naval career, for instance, Charles had little difficulty in persuading them to let him script and direct one small segment himself. While the major portion of the finished film had the traditional cap-tipping, knee-bending attitude the BBC invariably adopts towards royalty, the sequence which Charles masterminded was almost the reverse, a slice of mickey-taking, a sort of Keystone Cops episode with Charles as the little man who could do nothing right, not even wreak vengeance on his flying instructor. That other Charles—Chaplin—would have loved it.

At the same time as they chuckled at his antics, many viewers found themselves identifying with and sympathizing with him in his role of underdog while at the same time admiring a royal prince who could discard dignity to such an extent. The result was a big boost for the princely image. And because the image of monarchy is no more than the combined images of those who represent it, a boost for that too.

Not before time. Over the previous decade the image of Britain's monarchy had tended to lose its glitter. With the Queen and her husband now in their middle years, they no longer—as Philip himself pointed out—had the same shining appeal as they had done when they were younger and the Queen was fresh to the throne.

Then suddenly there was Prince Charles to enliven the scene, no longer a shy, blushing, foot-shuffling boy, but a tall. athletic young man oozing confidence, at one and the same time dashing, joky and sensitive, a princely model for other young men to emulate, for girls to kiss and their mums to drool over. For the monarchy the whole thing could hardly have happened at a better time if it had been pre-packaged by a team of public relations experts.

If there was a danger at one time that the gossip columns might overdo the lover-boy image, marriage has effectively put a stop to that. The truth is that Charles was never a philandering play-boy in the sense that the term could have been applied to the great-uncle who was Prince of Wales before him. There is in him no sign of the wayward streak there was in the Duke of Windsor in youth. Instead, he is almost a reincarnation—or so his grandmother thinks—of Windsor's dutiful younger brother who had monarchy thrust upon him and against the odds made a magnificent job of it.

Like his dead grandfather, Charles is dutiful and conscientious, hard-working in the cause of monarchy. His grandfather worked himself to death as King. If necessary, Charles would do the same. And in the new Princess of Wales he has surely found the right partner for his life's work.

2 Child

Because his parents, not yet married quite a full year, still lacked a proper home of their own, the future Prince of Wales, like his mother before him, was born in the home of his maternal grandparents. In his case, because those grandparents happened to be King George VI and Queen Elizabeth, the home in question was Buckingham Palace. The date was 14th November 1948, a Sunday. It was fourteen minutes past nine in the evening, according to the official announcement, when the latest in the royal line weighed in at 7 pounds 6 ounces.

He was not only King George VI's first grandchild, but as the firstborn son of the elder of the King's two daughters, next to his mother in the line of succession and almost certainly a future king, thirty-ninth in descent from Alfred the Great. Death apart, only two things

58

could ever oust him from his birthright: the unlikely possibility that his grandfather might yet have a son of his own and a latter-day upsurge of republicanism in Britain.

The first of these, as we know, did not happen. The second was not even a cloud on the horizon in that immediate postwar era. On the contrary, in a Britain where words such as 'nationalization' and 'inflation' were almost without meaning, in which the trade unions had not yet flexed their industrial muscles and become an alternative government, the birth was greeted with a wave of national emotion which would have justified the Second Coming. In the hours preceding the baby's birth the crowds almost stormed the palace gates in a fervour of loyal enthusiasm. In the hours immediately following, the royal switchboard was in danger of burning out under the influx of congratulatory telephone calls. It took two titled physicians, two more who did not yet possess a title and a hard-working midwife to effect the delivery which palace servants hailed with rapturous cries of 'It's a boy,' though the official announcement subsequently made it carefully clear that the then Princess Elizabeth had in fact been 'safely delivered of a Prince'.

A Prince then at birth, but nothing more. Some of his other titles were to come later, on the death of his grandfather; more still on his creation as schoolboy Prince of Wales. And only just a Prince. Had he been born even a week earlier, as royal physicians had at one time calculated he might be, there would have been no title, princely status being limited at that time (through a decree issued years before by King George V) to the sons of a king's son. Just in time his grandfather realized the danger that his grandchild might be raised as a commoner and a royal edict, a bare five days before the birth, saw the status of Prince extended also to any sons born to the King's elder daughter.

Prince or boy, there were some who reacted as though the birth was the result of some sort of divine dispensation rather than a mere natural process. 'We all knew the Princess wouldn't let us down. We all knew she'd have a son', one enthused onlooker solemnly assured others in the vast crowd outside the palace. Looking back more than quarter of a century, it perhaps seems a little absurd, certainly tribal, that the fountains in Trafalgar Square should display a blue rinse, guns bang away in Hyde Park, bonfires blaze on distant hilltops, old ladies ruin their eyesight knitting gifts of baby clothes and the Poet Laureate break out into a few lines of not very inspiring verse to mark the fact that an island kingdom was assured of its next chieftain. And yet the whole business will almost certainly be repeated all over again, and the crowds be just as thick and excitable if not thicker and even more excitable, at such time as the new Princess of Wales gives birth to a future heir to the throne.

The baby was christened in the white and gold Music Room of the palace. The ceremony was performed by the Archbishop of Canterbury and the holy water employed for the purpose had been specially imported from the River Jordan. The silk and lace robe in which the babe was swaddled had been handed down from Queen Victoria's day and the gold font had been originally designed by the old Queen's beloved Prince Albert for the christening of their own firstborn. In the line-up of official sponsors, those on the maternal side rather outnumbered and out-ranked those from the father's side, including as they did the baby's grandfather, King George VI; his great-grandmother, Queen Mary; his aunt, Princess Margaret; and a great-uncle, David Bowes-Lyon; as against Philip's grandmother, the Dowager Marchioness of Milford Haven, and his cousin, Lady Brabourne (the former Patricia Mount-batten). Two others—King Haakon of Norway and Prince George of Greece—were represented by proxies.

The baby was named Charles for no other reason than that the parents liked the name. 'Now I suppose I'll be known as Charley's aunt,' Princess Margaret giggled. Other names were added for various reasons: Philip because it was the name of the baby's father and George after grandfather George VI. With Queen Victoria so long dead, no longer any need to fuss over whether or not to include the name of her beloved Albert. Instead, Arthur was slipped in.

No one at the time appears to have given much thought to the fact that, in accordance with the normal British custom whereby children take their father's surname, the baby had been born a Mountbatten, the anglicized version of the German Battenberg which Philip had borrowed from his mother's side of the family at the time he became a British national. It was only later, on the death of King George VI and the accession of Princess Elizabeth as Queen Elizabeth II, that the matter assumed importance. Philip might be the father, but mother was now the Queen. Even in those pre-women's lib days, clearly she outranked him. Hence her Order in Council on 9th April 1952, some two months after her accession, made—it is said—on the insistence of her Prime Minister, Winston Churchill.

This Order declared it as her 'Will and Pleasure that I and my children shall be styled and known as the House and Family of Windsor and that my descendants, other than female descendants who marry and their descendants, shall bear the name of Windsor.'

I and my children.... So young Charles Mountbatten, then three years old, became Charles Windsor.

In the years which followed the Queen was to feel that, in accepting Churchill's advice and following her own desire to perpetuate her father's and grandfather's adopted name of Windsor, she had been less than fair to the man she married. Hence her further Order in Council on 8th February 1960, amending the previous one. This second Order in Council declared it now to be her 'Will and Pleasure that, while I and my children shall continue to be styled and known as the House and Family of Windsor, my descendants other than descendants enjoying the style, title or attribute of Royal Highness and the titular dignity of Prince or Princess and female descendants who marry and their descendants, shall bear the name of Mountbatten-Windsor.'

Under this new Order in Council, Charles Windsor who had been born Charles Mountbatten now became

Charles Mountbatten-Windsor.

You don't quite understand? Nor, at the time, did some of those considered authorities on the subject.

It was, as we said in our earlier book *The Crown And The Ring,* 'a cumbersomely worded and perhaps ambiguous declaration'. Concerned with the niceties of law, the one thing it did not do was make abundantly clear exactly what the Queen wanted. Realizing this, the Queen decided to issue a simultaneous explanatory statement:

'The Queen has always wanted, without changing the name of the royal house established by her grandfather, to associate the name of her husband with her own and his descendants.'

How much simpler if she had said simply: 'I want all my children to be called Mountbatten-Windsor in future.' But she didn't, and even the explanatory statement left a lot of people puzzled.

Writing in the *Daily Express* at the time, the then editor of *Debrett,* Cyril Hankinson, interpreted the situation as follows:

'It is most unlikely that there will ever

be a Mountbatten-Windsor dynasty. But this is how it could come about:

'If the Queen's third baby were a Prince....*

'If the Prince married and had a son who was created a Duke and the son then had two sons. The elder son would then take one of his father's secondary titles and would not then need a surname, but the younger son would be a Mountbatten-Windsor...

'If the line of the Prince of Wales became extinct...

'If the Mountbatten-Windsor's elder brother died without issue...

'Then the Mountbatten-Windsor would succeed to the throne. It is as remote as that.'

However, another authority, the late Edward Iwi, took a somewhat different view. Writing in the *Law Journal* (18th March 1960), this was his analysis:

'Reading the words of the Declaration and message together, as we are entitled to do, and bearing in mind that they were

---

*IT WAS. PRINCE ANDREW, BORN 19TH FEBRUARY 1960

given out on the same day and only eleven days before the birth of the infant Prince (Andrew), we may well feel that the Queen intended the name Mountbatten-Windsor to be in the lineage of her children, not merely to be given to her great-grandchildren and their descendants. To give the Royal children the name of Mountbatten-Windsor—even if they never use it—is in keeping with the idea that it is the birth-right of every legitimate child in a Christian country to be identified with its father.'

It would be space-consuming, and perhaps boring to all but a few, to re-iterate Iwi's legal argument in full. Skipping all that, we come to this: 'Reading the Queen's Declaration in conjunction with the contemporaneous message and in the light of the surrounding circumstances, the writer feels that the conclusion is patently clear. While sympathizing with the difficulties of cautious presentation felt by the draftsman, working perhaps at speed, it is yet natural to interpret the Declaration simply as intimating that Her Majesty's real intention was to confer upon each of her children what has been, so the writer believes, properly described as a 'hidden surname'.

'The common man using his common sense will arrive at the same conclusion as most lawyers. They will understand the 1960 Declaration to be that the Queen's House and Family is named Windsor; that of her children if they ever use a family name after their Christian names would be Mountbatten-Windsor, and it is that name which they will pass on to their descendants and which will be used by those descendants when the use of a surname becomes necessary.'

Iwi's interpretation has turned out to be the correct one. Out of love and loyalty to her husband, the Queen wanted her children to bear his name of Mountbatten while at the same time preserving her own family name of Windsor. Herself confused by all the argument surrounding the matter, she later, we are told, consulted the Lord Chancellor. He advised her that her own wish in the matter was what really counted. If she wanted her children to be Mountbatten-Windsors, then that was that. As a result,

Princess Anne, when she married Mark Phillips on 14th November 1973, did so in the name of 'Anne Mountbatten-Windsor'.

And Prince Charles, we are informed by Buckingham Palace, will be designated in the same fashion 'at such time as he needs to use his name'.

And what about that perhaps distant day when he succeeds to the throne as King Charles III? Says Buckingham Palace: 'He will still reign as a member of the House of Windsor unless he himself wishes to change things at that time.'

All this, of course—even the first change of name from Mountbatten back to Windsor—was still very much in the future at the time the baby prince was being wheeled around in an old-fashioned, high-bodied baby carriage, hoarded and handed down with the economy the Royals display in some directions, though not in others, from his mother's own childhood. Charles has said that he can actually recall such outings, a quite remarkable feat of royal memory. We wonder if he also recalls the elderly royal servant who had only so

69

much as to glimpse the baby carriage, whether or not she could see its small occupant, to be thrown into such a fit of vapours that she would bob a sustained curtsey.

The Queen, shortly after the births of Andrew and Edward, was once heard to remark that she had 'made mistakes' in the upbringing of Prince Charles and did not intend to repeat them with her two youngest children. Exactly what she meant by that it is, of course, impossible to know. Probably, as we shall see presently, she was thinking of the extreme publicity to which Charles was exposed throughout his childhood and schoolboy years. But there were perhaps also other 'mistakes' even if the Queen herself did not—and perhaps does not even now—see them as such. Throughout his babyhood and early boyhood the young Charles was treated with a degree of veneration which could hardly help but give him the idea that he was someone special. His mother, if she discouraged this in some directions, encouraged it, however unwittingly, in others, bridling slightly when well-meaning people inquired how 'the baby' was coming along. They really ought to refer to her son as His Royal Highness, she felt.

Children are very much the products of their environment and it is hardly surprising that the young Charles should soon come to regard himself in the same elevated light, even to the extent of seeking to correct Nanny Lightbody the day portrait painter Stella Marks visited the royal nursery.

'That's Charles,' said Nanny Lightbody, displaying a photograph.

'That's *Prince* Charles,' a small voice corrected her. He was two at the time.

The amount of nursery over-manning deemed necessary to raise one small boy, once the family had moved into a home of their own at Clarence House, would be hard to justify even in one of today's nationalized industries. Top of the nursery tree came Nanny Lightbody. First name, Helen; courtesy title, Mrs; an Edinburgh Scot. Under her came Mabel Anderson, though she, in all fairness, was to devote the major portion of her energies to sister Anne, born on 15th August 1950. In the best traditions of

British nanny-dom, neither she nor Mrs Lightbody could be expected to do the more menial tasks, of course. This necessitated the further assistance of two housemaids, though only one was on duty at a time. For the heavier chores there was a nursery footman. There was a detective to trail after the baby carriage when Charles was taken out for an airing, though in those less violent times neither he nor Nanny Lightbody raised any objection if some passing stranger requested the privilege of a peep at the sleeping bairn. There was, after Anne's birth, a nursery maid to help out further with the chores and, later still, a governess to give the boy his first lessons. There was a Miss Vacani to instruct him in dancing and deportment and a Miss Bor to give him piano lessons. With so many people bobbing, ducking and weaving around him, it is perhaps hardly to be wondered at that Charles, at this early stage of his young life, should come to regard himself as someone rather special. Not, of course, that he had any basis for comparison. Indeed, for years to come he appeared to think that all children were privileged to be brought up by nannies. 'Are you their nanny?' he was to ask a surprised woman with two small children whom he met in a mining village during his investiture tour of Wales.

His upbringing, in early years, followed the accepted royal pattern. His mother would nurse and play with him for perhaps half an hour after breakfast each morning. Royal duties permitting, she would visit the nursery at lunchtime to check on him or take him out for an airing in the Clarence House garden during the afternoon. She would visit the nursery again in the evening, when she would spend perhaps an hour and a half playing with him, reading to him, giving him his bath and finally tucking him down for the night. But she did not have him around her, under her feet, at all hours of the day, as most young mothers do. She did not have to wash him and dress him in the morning, change him at intervals during the course of the day and prepare his food at mealtimes. Or if she did, it was only occasionally and because she felt like doing it. She did not have to struggle sleepy-eyed from bed to see to him if he was fretful at night. As he grew from babyhood to childhood, she taught him to write his name, that c-a-t spells 'cat' and how to tell the time. She gave him his first lessons in those other two essentials of royalty, politeness and punctuality, but she did not have to wash, iron, patch or darn his clothes. She did not have to scrub behind his ears, haul him round the shops with her or lament the fact that there was no one else to take over from her and keep him amused on a wet day. Yet while she did less for him, saw less of him, than would have been the case in an ordinary family, a special 'closeness' was to develop between mother and son which still exists today. Perhaps it is the constant close contact in ordinary families which sometimes leads later to misunderstanding, even friction, between parents and children, what has become known as 'the generation gap'. Between Charles and his parents no such 'gap' has ever existed.

Except at weekends and holiday times, mother and child saw each other for perhaps no more than three hours a day, if that. So, for each of them, their hours together were something of a treat rather than mere routine, the more so because there were times when the then Princess Elizabeth, flying out to see Philip in Malta (where he was serving in the Navy) or busy with the increasing number of royal chores which came her way as her father's health deteriorated, did not see her small son for days on end. Occasionally there was even a gap of a week or two. And she was to see even less of him when, with her father's premature death, the whole burden of monarchy was thrown suddenly upon her young shoulders. Even when he went down with chicken pox she could not nurse him herself as most other mothers do their children. She was now the Queen and must not be exposed to the risk of possible infection.

So Charles, at this stage of his young life, was left largely to the care of Nanny Lightbody. Neither he, she nor his parents saw anything extraordinary in this. It was, to them, a perfectly normal way of life. The nursery apartment—a day nursery, bathroom, a kitchen added later on Philip's suggestion and two night nurseries, one shared by Charles and Mrs Lightbody, the other by Anne and Mabel Anderson—was like a self-contained world of its own. In this small world with its chintz curtains and matching armchairs, its applewood table for meals and its glass-fronted cabinet containing china and silver miniatures, Mrs Lightbody reigned supreme. As in most upper-class nurseries, mother might lay down the broad principles of her child's upbringing but she did not interfere in the day-to-day management. Even the daily timetable for parental visits to the children was arranged by agreement with Mrs Lightbody and, later, when Charles and Anne were of an age to go to their mother's sitting-room at the end of her working day instead of her visiting the nursery, they were supposed to be back in the nursery for supper at quarter past seven sharp. If they were not, the meal was put on the table for them just the same. The Queen, for the most part, abided by the nursery rule. The Queen Mother, if she had charge of the children while her daughter was away, was less of a clock-watcher.

But if the nursery was Nanny Lightbody's little kingdom, it can hardly be said that she ruled it with an iron hand. The Duke of Windsor, when he was a child, may have had a nanny who would sometimes twist his arm for the pleasure of seeing him in tears when he was taken down to see his parents. Mrs Lightbody would never even have dreamed of doing such a thing. She doted on her small charge, petting him, spoiling him, going to the other extreme so that he began to grow up a rather precocious and timid little boy.

'He was never as boisterous or noisy as Princess Anne,' Mabel Anderson has recalled. 'She had a much stronger, more extrovert personality. She didn't exactly push him aside, but she was certainly a more forceful child. He was basically a rather shy little boy.'

His parents, when he was with them, were less concerned than Mrs Lightbody to shield him from the small knocks of growing up. On holiday with them, blackberrying at Balmoral or romping about the beach at Holkham, near Sandringham, he was permitted to behave like any other small boy, running about, falling down, getting grubby and tousled. But within the confines of the royal nursery he was always a small Prince, to be treated as such and expected to behave as such. The games of boyhood were out if they involved any risk of being hurt, getting dirty or the possibility of lowering princely dignity. Charles was not yet four when, up and about before Nanny Lightbody one morning, he came across a footman making an early-morning pot of tea. Boy-like he wanted to help. After that it became something of a game for him to hurry along to the footman's room and help with the tea-making each morning. Then Mrs Lightbody came to hear about it and the 'game' was discontinued.

There were occasionally opportunities for letting off boyish steam, particularly when Philip was home—improvised football games with father in the wide corridor flanking the royal apartment after the move back to Buckingham Palace, boisterous pillow fights at bedtime. As Mabel Anderson has recalled: 'The Duke was marvellous. He always used to set aside time to read to the children or put together those little model toys with them. Princess Anne was very good at model-making, but not Prince Charles—all fingers and thumbs.'

There were toys galore, of course—a model of Gibraltar complete with working railway; a rocking-horse minus its tail handed down from the days of his mother's childhood; a big box of dressing-up clothes; a marvellous miniature car to be raced round and round the Grand Hall of the palace; toboggans shaped like flying saucers for both him and Anne one Christmas. There were pets—the corgi pups, Whisky and Sherry; a rabbit named Harvey; a pair of lovebirds called Annie and Davy (after sharp-shooting Annie Oakley and Davy Crockett); and a hamster named Chi-Chi (which his mother detested). But Anne apart, there were no playmates of his own age. Politeness was drilled into him to such an extent that both he and Anne said 'Please' even to their pet corgis when trying to teach them tricks. He was taught to shake hands and utter a polite

'Hello, I'm Charles' when visitors came to call. He even stuck out a small hand in greeting when he was first reunited with his mother at the end of the six-month round-the-world tour which followed her coronation. The Queen was horrified. She was even more horrified the time he bowed to her on entering her sitting-room while Anne bobbed a curtsey; so horrified that she broke the unwritten rule about not interfering with nursery routine. There would be no more bowing or curtseying by her children, she said.

Practical jokes were tolerated by Mrs Lightbody, encouraged by his parents. Indeed, many of them originated with the boy's father. Practical joking would seem to run in the Royal Family. Edward VII, when he was Prince of Wales, thought it a great joke to pop things like dead seagulls into other people's beds, though preferring something livelier and warmer in his own. The Duke of Windsor once fed an unsuspecting visitor a tadpole sandwich. Charles' jokes were less unpleasant and quite harmless, an imitation ink blot on the sitting-room carpet, a fearsome-looking toy spider, a gadget to make tea-plates bob up and down. He also had a rude-noise cushion which had to be hastily removed from a window seat at Sandringham on one occasion just as the visiting Bishop of Norwich was about to sit on it.

His isolation from the outside world continued with lessons in the nursery schoolroom. Anne, when her turn for lessons came later, was to have other girls for company. Andrew and Edward, later still, were to have a co-ed education even in nursery days. But Charles, until Anne joined him, was the lonely only child in a class of one.

His governess, Katharine Peebles, was to remember him later as a sensitive, rather nervous child. 'If you raised your voice to him, he would draw back into his shell and for a time you would be able to do nothing with him. He liked being amused rather than amusing himself.'

Lessons in the nursery schoolroom, like all the rest of his young life, were largely conditioned by the specialness of his royal background. He might know all about the geography of his mother's travels, but, as schoolmates at Hill House soon realized when he went to school there later, he did not know the difference in value between a penny and a two-shilling piece. How could he? He had been in a shop only about twice in his life and even then Miss Peebles had counted out his money for him. His mother, incidentally, had much the same sort of problem when she helped out at a charity sale-of-work one summer shortly after her accession to the throne. A lady-in-waiting had to help her work out the change.

Until he went to Hill House, Charles had hardly any knowledge of or contact with the ordinary world beyond the palace railings. Worse still, he had too little contact with the world of boyhood. Except for an occasional meeting with relatives at holiday times, he had no other boys with whom to play. Indeed, the only males with whom he had more or less regular contact were his father (who was away a good deal of the time), the young nursery footman and the groom who gave him his riding lessons. And fraternization with the last two beyond what was necessary was hardly encouraged.

All else around him was female...his mother, his small, more dominating sister, his nanny, his governess. And if his mother was away, then it was over to Granny, who was also inclined to indulge and spoil him, and Aunt Margo. It was an upbringing which was top-heavy in two directions. With so many adults so constantly around him, he was becoming grown-up and precocious beyond his years. With so much petticoat government ordering his young life, he had little chance, shy and sensitive as he was by nature, of developing into a real boy.

Busy as she was in so many other directions during those early years of her monarchy, away so much, uncritically delighted simply to be with her children when opportunity served, the Queen did not notice what was happening. Perhaps she would not have recognized it for what it was even if she had. But Philip did.

Brought up in a considerably less restricted, more independent fashion, shuffled from school to school in France, England, Germany and Scotland during the years of his boyhood, Philip not only saw what was happening but knew that this was not the way he wanted a son of his brought up. One cannot know, of course, what he may have said to his wife within the privacy of the family circle, but that he said something is apparent from the subtle change in direction which now took place with regard to Charles' upbringing. The first small pointer to Philip's decision that the boy should be raised more in his own thrusting, extrovert, athletic image was the temporary engagement of a male tutor. Music lessons were cut down and dancing lessons discontinued altogether. On the afternoons thus made available Charles was hauled off to a playing field in Chelsea where he punted a football about with other boys of his own age and to a private gymnasium where he embarked upon a course of light exercises designed to stretch and toughen young muscles.

All this he found enjoyable and exciting enough. But he was extremely upset when, as the next link in the chain of change, Nanny Lightbody was suddenly retired (though Mabel Anderson was kept on to look after Anne) and shunted off to a Duchy of Cornwall grace-and-favour apartment not far from the Oval cricket ground. His distress at her departure is understandable. Until now she had been almost like a second mother to him. Indeed, he had seen rather more of her over the years of his childhood than of his actual mother. She had washed him, fed him, played with him, praised him when he was good, consoled him when he was sad, punished him (by not letting him watch television) on the rare occasions he was naughty, and even slept in the same room with him at night. All this had forged a link between them which it was a wrench to break and which, in fact, was not to be entirely broken. Years later, as a young man, he called round one day to have a cup of tea with her in her flat near the Oval and, when the time came for his investiture as Prince of Wales, he saw to it that she had a seat at the ceremony.

But between the two events—Nanny Lightbody's departure and his investiture as Prince of Wales eleven years later—was to come the ordeal of school-days.

In many ways, Charles' first experience of school life was a suitably soft-centre interlude between the cotton-wool cushioning of the royal nursery and the rough and tumble of boarding school life which was to come later. The teachers at Hill House, a private day school in the Knightsbridge area of London, were mostly female. One at least remembers him as 'a rather nervous little boy'. Lessons were relatively relaxed and his first school report recorded that he 'loves' history, was 'very good' at reading, 'good' at writing, geography, art and gymnastics, showed promise in French, had made 'only a fair start' at Latin and, like his mother before him, was 'not very keen' on arithmetic.

To his parents, all this was satisfactory enough. Even more satisfactory, to his father, was the fact that the process of making a man of him instead of merely a Prince had finally started. But school-days were also to create a situation new to Buckingham Palace and one with which neither the Royals nor their advisers really knew how to cope. Their failure to do so was perhaps one of the 'mistakes' the Queen feels she made in the upbringing of her eldest son. And for Charles, throughout much of his schooldays, it resulted in what his mother has referred to as 'terrible times'.

The royal marriage, the births of two children, the King's tragic death, the Queen's accession and coronation...all these things, following hard on the heels of each other over the short space of less than six years, had combined to arouse in Britain a fever of loyal emotion that was little short of deification. It was to be seen in the vast crowds which besieged Buckingham Palace in the hours before and immediately following Charles' birth. It even broke out on one occasion in the remote royal fastness of Balmoral where a marquee was ripped apart and people trampled on each other in their frantic desire to see the Royals act as stallholders at a church jumble sale. It revealed itself also in the letters of well-meaning advice and the packets of cure-alls which descended on Buckingham Palace if word got round that Charles or

Anne was down with the snuffles. Newspapers and magazines, scenting the possibility of increased circulations, were not slow to cater to the national fervour. The spread of television intensified the whole business. Reporters and photographers dogged the Royals almost wherever they went, and none more so than young Charles. Telephoto lenses intruded upon royal privacy and what Prince Philip was to condemn as 'keyhole' gossip about their personal lives became almost the order of the day. Royal servants were not above purveying items of interest (for a suitable consideration) and one freelance photographer found that he could achieve a worthwhile income by stalking the Royal Family wherever they went and selling the results of his efforts worldwide. With the exception of a few of the more esoteric publications, everyone was frantic to get in on the act and some of the things published at the time were silly to the point of downright absurdity, as when the *Tailor & Cutter* ranked the boy Charles (he was six at the time) top of the best-dressed men of the year on account of his 'Baby-

Bow and Fawn Stalker followed by his junior fashion for a double-breasted Woolly'. To say nothing, of course, of his 'velvet-collared topcoat'.

The royal parents did what they could to check the harassment of their son. When Charles, prior to going to Hill House, was sent on a series of visits to places like Westminster Abbey, the Tower of London and the Science Museum, the Queen appealed to the press and public to calm things down and give the boy a break. She wanted her son, she said, to be able to enjoy such outings 'in the same way as other children can without the embarrassment of constant publicity'. Her motherly appeal had only small effect and none at all during the first few days Charles was at Hill House. The school was already under siege by photographers, reporters and eager-beaver sightseers when he arrived on the first day in his off-the-peg blazer and cap. That, perhaps, was only to be expected. It was the first time in British history that an heir to the throne had ever gone to school and public interest was understandable. But when the third day of his schooling came with no sign of any let-up—if anything, interest and pressure seemed to be increasing—his mother put her foot down. As mother, she refused to let him leave for school until word reached her that the bulk of the crowd milling round Hill House had apparently given up hope of seeing him that day and had begun to disperse. As Queen, she had her press secretary telephone the editors of various national newspapers and ask them to call their men off. They did, but the respite, as we shall see, was only temporary.

3   Schoolboy*

Picture a rather plump little chap of nine, his hair a bit on the long side for those pre-Beatles days, away from his several homes (Buckingham Palace, Windsor Castle, Balmoral Castle and the 'Big House' at Sandringham) for almost the first time in his life, sitting miserably on a rather spartan bed consisting of a flock mattress perched on wooden slats in an unheated dormitory with the floor of bare boards (so different from the carpeted comfort of the royal nursery), fighting back tears as he nibbles his nails and nurses the large box of chocolates given to him by his parents as a going-away present. Shyness rather than greediness prevents him sharing his chocs with the other nine boys in the dorm.

This, then, was Charles on his first night at Cheam, a boarding school for

*APPENDIX II

boys, the same one—though not in the same place, having moved from Surrey to Hampshire since the 1930s—which his father had gone to around the same age.

The idea that Charles should be buzzed off to boarding school was largely Prince Philip's. Left to her own devices, still advised at that time by the old guard of royal aides who had advised her father before her, the Queen would almost certainly never have thought of it. Why should she? Except for a few day trips from Windsor Castle to Eton College for lessons in constitutional history and suchlike, she herself had never been to school. Nor had her sister, Princess Margaret. Nor their mother. Nor their father (though he did spend a year at Trinity College, Cambridge, where Charles was also to go later); nor his father; nor any other heir to the throne in Britain's long history.

So, from the Queen's point of view, it was almost a revolutionary experiment. If it did not go quite as far as some other people may have wished, it was still a very considerable step in the right direction, a move away from the continued rarefied upbringing he would have had if educated by private tutors. Of course there were those, like the then Lord Altrincham, who would have preferred the boy to have been tossed in at the deep end of state schooling. Heaven only knows what his young life would have been like if his parents had listened to that sort of argument. It was to be miserable enough at times even in the more exclusive fee-paying surroundings of a privately-run boarding school.

The Queen, in deciding to send Charles to Cheam, perhaps saw it as a way of shielding him from the glare of the public spotlight. Philip had other reasons. Boarding school, he felt, was the best way of moulding Charles into the sort of son he most wanted him to be.

Initially, father was to be disappointed. There was little sign of any real metamorphosis during Charles' early days at Cheam. Most small boys, of course, are miserable and insecure when they are first torn from the bosoms of their families and pitchforked into the hurly-burly of boarding school life. But most adapt quickly enough, get over the upset and settle down. Charles did not. He dreaded the idea of boarding school before ever he went to Cheam; was thoroughly miserable when he got there; had only just begun to settle down when it was time to move on to Gordonstoun; was even more wretched at Gordonstoun when he first went there. And later, while he may no longer have been unhappy at Gordonstoun, it cannot honestly be said that he was completely happy either. Instead, he was—his own word—'bored'.

Yet, oddly, the experiment—at least, from Philip's point of view—somehow succeeded. And looking back, the loneliness and unhappiness of much of his schooldays now blurred by the passage of time, Charles today is conscious perhaps only of the benefits. His schooldays disciplined him; taught him self-reliance; encouraged him to rise to—even welcome—challenge. In brief, however much he may have detested them at the time, they did much towards making him the man he has become.

There were a number of reasons—and perhaps two salient reasons—why Charles never completely settled down at

94

either Cheam or Gordonstoun; why he was never completely happy at either establishment. That he should have found schoolboy life unsettling when he first went to Cheam, very different from anything he had known before, is surely understandable. No longer was Nanny Lightbody around to pet and comfort him, to fold his clothes and tidy his things. No longer was there a housemaid to make his bed and a footman to clean his shoes for him. All these things—bed-making, shoe-cleaning, clothes-folding —he was now required to do for himself. No longer did he have a room of his own, a bathroom of his own. Instead, he had to share with a bunch of other—pushing, shoving, first-come-first-served—youngsters. No longer was there someone to wait on him at mealtimes. Instead, there were even times when he found himself waiting on others.

It was all very different from what had gone before, some of it novel and exciting, much of it frightening and nerve-racking. And to all of it, with the resilience of boyhood, Charles would adjust in due course. But there were other problems of schooldays which he would never fully resolve.

Prince Philip has said many times that his own schooldays were among the happiest of his life. In sending his son to the same schools that had moulded him in boyhood, he clearly anticipated that Charles would enjoy them just as much. But Charles was not Philip. His nature was not his father's nature. And even Philip, an almost unknown Royal of whom very few people had heard until he stepped into the limelight as the future husband of the future Queen, might well have found his own schooldays much tougher, more of a strain, less happy, had he been under the same pressures young Charles found himself obliged to endure.

The public spotlight was one. By sending him to boarding school, the boy's mother, as we have said, hoped to ease the pressure on him in this direction. Her hopes were not fulfilled. On the contrary, Cheam was a quick and easy journey from London and the novelty of an heir to the throne sitting in class with ordinary boys was seen by the newspapers as justifying extra effort on their part. So photographers continued to stalk him, even following him into the school grounds; reporters questioned masters, school servants, other boys, anyone from whom some small titbit of gossip concerning the schoolboy Prince might be prised...like the fact that he found school meals too rich for his young stomach when he first went to Cheam.

Of his first eighty-eight days at Cheam, there were headlines about him in the national newspapers on sixty-eight days. The school authorities, though aware of what was happening, found themselves powerless to deal with the situation and turned to Buckingham Palace for help. The result was another royal appeal to editors and the general public to leave Charles alone and let Cheam get on with its task of educating him and his ninety small schoolmates. The appeal, if not completely heeded, did have some effect.

Anxious not to encourage further publicity through her own actions, the Queen visited the school no more frequently than any ordinary parent and perhaps less then most. Certainly she did not go dashing off to visit Charles in sick bay when he went down with the flu; nor when he injured himself in a fall and ended up hobbling around with one leg in plaster. 'Hopalong Cassidy' sister Anne labelled him when he went home, his leg still in plaster, for the Christmas vacation.

On the rare occasions when she did visit the school, the Queen asked to be treated like any other parent, a royal request which cut two ways and included not having cameras pointed at her. Ordinary parents, after all, are not photographed by the press or snap-shotted by other boys whenever they go to boarding school to visit their young son.

But if school and royal parents could recognize and do something about this particular problem, there was yet another problem which either they failed to understand or, if they did, were quite unable to do anything about. This second problem arose not from outside but from inside the school, stemming partly from Charles himself, partly from the other

Prince Charles with Nanny Lightbody watching the Royal procession on the way to the opening of Parliament, 1950

Below, left: The Prince on his third birthday with his grandfather King George VI

Below, right: Prince Charles and Princess Anne in the garden of Royal Lodge, Windsor in 1954

Wearing a kilt of the Balmoral tartan, the young Prince strolls round the grounds of Balmoral Castle

Prince Charles playing cricket during his second term at Hill House School in London

Prince Charles arriving at King's Cross Station, London,
after an overnight journey from Gordonstoun School

Prince Charles with his room-mate walking through the gum trees on their way to chapel at Timbertop, Australia

The Prince relaxing in his study at Trinity College, Cambridge

Prince Charles playing his part in rehearsals for one of the college revues at Cambridge

Greetings on arrival at the University College of Wales, Aberystwyth, 1969

The Queen proudly presenting her son, the new Prince of Wales, to the people of Wales from one of the battlements of Caernarvon Castle, July 1969

The Prince and his family, at home at Sandringham

Dancing with his cousin, Lady Sarah Armstrong-Jones

boys and partly also, though perhaps to a lesser degree, from some of the masters.

It arose for two main reasons. One was Charles' own timidity and shyness, handed down from his mother and grandfather, fostered by the cosseting of Nanny Lightbody. The other was the degree of awe with which, because he was the Queen's son, he was regarded by most of the other boys and some of the staff.

'It is the wish of the Queen and Prince Philip that...Prince Charles shall be treated exactly the same as the other boys', the school's joint headmasters, Peter Beck and Mark Wheeler, were at pains to point out in a circular letter which they sent to the parents of other pupils ahead of Charles' arrival. 'It would be a great help if you could explain this to your boys.'

But no amount of headmasterly pleading or parental explanation can alter basic human nature. To the other boys, Charles was 'different'...'special'...and in their varying ways they were bound to treat him as such. Some steered clear of him out of a sense of awe; others because they did not want it to be thought that they were trying to curry favour. Nor would his own shyness permit him to make those first all-important moves which might have led to friendship and for a time headmaster Beck's small daughter, Mary, a few months younger than Charles, was perhaps his most frequent companion.

Not every other boy ignored him of course. Inevitably there were one or two, as there are in every schoolboy collection, who thought it 'big' to taunt him, nicknaming him 'Fatty' because of his podginess, and even to bully him. The school authorities did not interfere. To have done so would have only made him seem more 'special' and made matters worse. He had to fight his own battles and there was one occasion when fighting back led to a schoolboy fracas for which Charles recalls being caned. If he did not suffer the indignities heaped upon the Duke of Windsor at the Royal Naval College, Osborne, where ink was poured over him and he was guillotined in a window frame as a reminder of what happened to Charles I, the future

Charles III did have his head dunked in cold water on one occasion. He retaliated vigorously enough to immerse his tormentor in a bath of water but rather spoilt the effect by overbalancing on top of him.

The school's headmasters were apparently unaware of his loneliness and, because of this, so were his parents. Not, perhaps, that they could have done anything about it even if they had known. So for a long time he remained a boy alone, shy, easily embarrassed, foot shuffling and nail nibbling, lonely in the midst of the schoolboy crowd. One of the school staff summed him up at the time: 'Shy, nervous, sometimes sullen, sometimes precocious'...four adjectives that have vanished with the years.

In time, of course, the ice of schoolboy relationships thawed slightly. He did make friends, but not many and never easily. With them, he was involved in one or two relatively mild Tom Brown-style japes. In accordance with his parents' idea that schooldays should be as 'ordinary' as possible, he travelled to and from Cheam at the beginning and end of each term by train with a bunch of other boys. He was allowed only the same amount of pocket money as other boys. And he was certainly not showered with ostentatious schoolboy gifts. The model yacht which he sailed on the school pond was among the smallest to be seen there. Academically, he proved no more than an average scholar, continuing good in geography (top of the class one term), art and French, but still weak at mathematics. He was good also at history, though one lesson revealed a surprising gap in his knowledge of his own family. He knew—or appeared to know—nothing of the short-reigned King Edward VIII who abdicated the throne for love of an American divorcee.

He enjoyed swimming at which he was extremely proficient; played cricket and football though without any great enthusiasm or any considerable success. Certainly he could not rival the athletic prowess his father had shown, years before, in setting a new high jump record. Though he made one or two friends, he remained acutely shy and easily embarrassed. It was always a considerable embarrassment to him to hear the preacher offer up prayers for the Duke of Cornwall and others of the Royal Family in church on Sunday mornings. He was even more embarrassed the time he was ushered into the headmaster's study, along with a bunch of school-fellows, to sit in front of a television set and watch the predominantly Welsh crowd at the Commonwealth Games in Cardiff cheer themselves hoarse at the announcement that he had been created Prince of Wales.*

Creating him Prince of Wales at so young an age, and while he was still at school, was perhaps one of the 'mistakes' his mother feels she made in his upbringing. It was, after all, a move in direct contradiction to the 'ordinary' upbringing she insisted she wanted for him. It had a number of results, none of them beneficial to him at this stage of his young life. It extended and increased the sense of awe with which he was largely regarded at Cheam; it did nothing to lessen his own sense of embarrassment at

*APPENDIX III

being 'different' from other boys; and it was, inevitably, the cause of a fresh outbreak of publicity about which the Queen could hardly complain when her own action was the cause of it.

All in all, the experiment of sending Charles to Cheam, though there were benefits, was not working out quite as his parents had visualized. Charles himself, later, was to give most of the credit for his metamorphosis from a nervous, precocious boy into a pleasantly modest and self-confident young man to the two terms he spent at school in Australia. Not everyone else would agree. While not denying the benefits of Timbertop, there are some who think that his spell at university played a perhaps even bigger part in his transformation. The fact is that what happened to him was no hey presto conjuring trick performed overnight in Australia (or in any other single place, come to that), but a slow, gradual process which, even if he was unaware of it, was already at work during those early years at Cheam. By the time he came to leave Cheam he had already lost at least some of his earlier precociousness and we have the word of someone who knew him at that time that there was also a small upsurge of schoolboy confidence. But not enough, unfortunately, to enable him to take the move from Cheam to Gordonstoun in his stride.

Charles was not quite fourteen when, still following in dad's footsteps, he left Cheam for Gordonstoun. It has been said that he himself took part in the family conference which led to Gordonstoun as the next step in the educational ladder. Maybe so, though it seems unlikely that, at thirteen and relatively unsure of himself still, he had very much to say in the matter and certainly nothing which could counter his father's enthusiasm for Gordonstoun. Given complete freedom of choice, Charles would perhaps have preferred to go to Charterhouse (though only because one of the few friends he had made at Cheam was going there).

Gordonstoun, in his parents' eyes, had several advantages. For one thing, it was in the north of Scotland, far from both the madding crowd and the clacking typewriters of Fleet Street. As we shall see, however, it was not far enough.

And while a long way from London, it was comparatively close to Balmoral, which might be useful. Another benefit, helpful when it came to making friends, was that he would have two schoolboy relatives there. But the biggest advantage of all, at least in his parents' eyes, was that Gordonstoun had also educated Philip in his day...and look at what it had done for him.

'I thoroughly enjoyed my days there,' Philip has said, and doubtless expected his son would do the same.

But Charles, at thirteen, rising fourteen, was by no means a carbon copy of what Philip had been at the same age... extrovert, athletic, almost arrogantly self-confident, a natural leader. He was still podgy rather than athletic, still almost painfully shy, and the small degree of new-won confidence he had gained towards the end of his time at Cheam was quickly to evaporate at his new school on the shore of the Moray Firth.

Even Philip, in boyhood, might have found his days at Gordonstoun less enjoyable had he gone there with the disadvantage of being son and heir to the world's best-known and most publicized monarch. 'I want you to treat him just like any other boy,' the Queen is supposed to have told Gordonstoun's headmaster when arranging for her son to go there. She may well have done so and Gordonstoun undoubtedly did its best to respond. It was perhaps no more than mere coincidence that the drive leading to the school was re-surfaced just prior to Charles' arrival and that Windmill Lodge, the house in which he would be quartered, was given a new lick of paint.

Coincidence or not, the other boys were quick to notice this spot of extra spit and polish, and as a result Charles was immediately labelled 'special'…'different'…just as he had been at Cheam. Through no fault of his own, he was off to a bad start.

Soon after he first went there, his father was asked how he was getting along at Gordonstoun. 'At least he hasn't run away yet', Philip replied, grinning.

Charles was not the type to run away

from school. Such an idea would never have occurred to him. But he did, soon after he went to Gordonstoun, ask the Queen Mother to intercede with his parents to take him away again.

Between Charles and his grandmother there has always existed a deep bond of affection and understanding. Most grandmothers, of course, have a special soft spot for the first of their grand-children. But with the Queen Mother it goes deeper than that. To her, Charles is the living image of the husband to whom she was so devoted throughout their years of marriage. In consequence, there was little she would not do for her grand-son if she could. Even if he could find no words beyond 'pretty gruesome' to convey to her what he thought of Gor-donstoun, she could see that he was unhappy there. Yet while she may have had private doubts as to whether Gordonstoun was the most suitable school for him, she felt she could not interfere with what his parents had decided. Instead, she did her best to explain to him that everyone, and perhaps particularly those who are born royal, have to do things in life they don't like. For Charles, Gordonstoun was one of those things.

Gordonstoun, in those days, had not yet gone co-educational. If it was perhaps not quite the spartan establishment legend would have us believe, it yet had about it almost an air of monasticism. It was no longer the small, compact collection of a few boys and masters it had been in Philip's day, where everyone knew everyone else, but a community of nearly four hundred boys with some forty-two masters and instructors. But the emphasis, as in Philip's day, was still more on character building than on either academic or athletic success. And what better way to build a boy's character than by putting him through a crowded and rugged itinerary which started with an early-morning jogtrot stripped to the waist followed by a quick cold shower. Crowded itineraries and cold showers, as is well known, also have a chastening effect on those fleshly temptations to which the male of the species is subject in puberty.

Gordonstoun's crowded routine left

little time to dwell on fleshly temptations. Starting with the quarter-to-seven
jogtrot and shower, it continued almost
non-stop through lessons (including two
in the evening), physical training, instruction in seamanship, army cadet training including a scaled-down commando
course, athletics and sports to prayers at
half-past eight at night and then lights
out. Various character-building chores
were thrown in for good measure. Twice
a week during his early days at Gordonstoun Charles found himself humping
the dustbins to their collecting point and
then clearing the area around of any
overflow scraps or waste paper. In turn
he was also detailed to clear away the
dirty plates at mealtimes, mow lawns,
weed flower beds and clean javelins, all
good character-building stuff. Discipline
was strict and there was one occasion,
after his locker was seen to be less neat
and tidy than Gordonstoun's high ideals
required, when he was given a spell of
PD (penalty drill). This involved going
round and round the south lawn, alter-
nately walking and running. If one of his
schoolmates can be believed, this was

one occasion when the future King did not quite rise to the school's *Plus est en vous* motto. Far from responding to the challenge of punishment, he slid surreptitiously out of the squad and hid in a convenient shrubbery until after the session.

Yet there were other occasions on which he did respond to challenge, showing that while he might not be a second Philip in all respects, there was one important quality he had inherited from his father and perhaps, on the other side of the family, from his dead grandfather also—guts.

One such occasion arose when he had been there only a few weeks. With a master to oversee them, he and eight other boys set off in one-man kayaks to paddle from nearby Hopeman Bay to Burghead, some two miles west. The weather at the outset was fine and all went so well initially that, reaching Burghead, it was decided to press on another six miles to Findhorn. Suddenly the weather changed, as it is apt to do in the Moray Firth. The wind freshened, the sea turned choppy and the rain belted down. What had been no more than a pleasant cruise became in a matter of minutes a hard slog. If there was perhaps no real danger, conditions were certainly bad enough to frighten young boys. Charles would be the last to claim that he does not know the meaning of fear. He has confessed to having had 'butterflies in the tummy' ahead of both his first solo flight and his later parachute jump. Almost certainly he experienced them also on that day in the Moray Firth. But he rose to the challenge and, when Findhorn was finally reached, had the satisfaction of feeling that, for perhaps the first time in his young life, he had achieved something really worthwhile.

In fact, his initial unhappiness at Gordonstoun was due less to the congestion and ruggedness of the school's itinerary than to the attitude of his schoolfellows and indeed of some of the masters who, in their determination to show that they were not favouring him because he was who he was, were sometimes inclined to go to the other extreme. There was one master whose displays of non-favouritism included addressing him merely as 'Windsor' and sometimes, in moments of sarcasm, even as 'Charlie boy'. Even so, Charles preferred this to the fawning obsequiousness displayed by some other masters. It at least made him feel that he really was one of the chaps.

As at Cheam, he did not find it easy to make friends. At Gordonstoun, however, he had two friends right from the outset, his German cousin, Guelf, the fifteen-year-old son of Prince Philip's sister, Princess Sophie of Hanover, and Norton Knatchbull, the son of Philip's cousin, Lady Brabourne (the former Patricia Mountbatten). But other boys with whom he would perhaps have liked to be friends were inclined to steer clear of him, as at Cheam, for fear that they would be accused of sucking up to him. It took Prince Alexander of Yugoslavia a long time to live down the nickname of 'Sponge' with which he was tagged after being detailed to show Charles round the school on his first day there. Those who did attempt to bridge the gap between themselves and the Queen's son were usually and almost inevitably the rather more brash youngsters and, rightly or wrongly, Charles mistrusted their motives.

As he explained years later: 'You would hear them accusing each other of sucking up and this was a problem. It's one of the things you learn through experience—how to sense the ones who are sucking up and those who are genuine. The trouble is that very often the worst people come up first and the really nice ones hang back because they don't want to be accused of sucking up.'

With the 'really nice ones' who were inclined to hang back, his own shyness prevented him from making the first move towards friendship. And though he did eventually make a few friends in addition to Guelf and Norton Knatchbull, he remained very much a loner during his early years at Gordonstoun, often drifting about with only his ever-present personal detective for company.

The spotlight of publicity continued to pursue him and never more so than the winter he went to Switzerland with Guelf and Guelf's brother, George, to learn to ski. Since those days the Royals have mastered the knack of keeping their personal lives reasonably private. Similar trips in more recent years for the younger members of the family, Andrew and Edward, have been planned and carried out with a fair degree of subterfuge and secrecy. Andrew, for instance, enjoyed an exchange visit to France on one occasion under the pseudonym of Andrew Edwards. Charles has similarly resorted to the use of cover names upon occasion, booking himself a sleeping berth on an overnight train to Scotland in the unlikely name of 'Mr Postle', calling himself Charles Windsor during a visit to a restaurant in Melbourne and signing himself into a working men's club while at Cambridge in the name of 'Charlie Chester'. After all, as he pointed out, his name is Charles and one of his titles is Earl of Chester.

But in those days such deviousness had not entered into royal thinking and he had no such *alter ego* protection on that ski-ing holiday in Switzerland. Wherever he went he was besieged by a crowd of sightseers and trailed by photographers. The more daring of the photographers even invaded the private grounds of the relatives' villa at which he was staying until finally the local police had to be called in. After that Charles continued his ski lessons within the privacy of the estate with three strapping Swiss policemen on skis detailed to keep the photographers and others at bay. There was to be further and more traumatic publicity during the years he remained at Gordonstoun.

In sending him to Gordonstoun, his parents had hoped that the school's comparative isolation and the 534 miles which separated it from Fleet Street would ensure that publicity was kept to a minimum. To protect him further, his mother, at the outset, had again appealed to the newspapers to leave him alone. He would derive 'full benefit from his days at school only if he is not made the centre of special attention', said a statement on her behalf. To a large degree, editors respected this royal request, but it would not have been in the nature of newspapers for them to have ignored the affair of the cherry brandy when it was handed to them almost on a silver salver.

Charles had been at Gordonstoun for rather more than a year when he was picked as one of the schoolboy crew for a training cruise aboard the *Pinta,* one of the school's two ketches. In the course of the cruise the vessel arrived in Stornoway on the Isle of Lewis where Charles went ashore with a handful of other boys. Inevitably he was recognized almost as soon as he set foot on dry land. A crowd gathered round and his personal detective, a young man named Donald Green, quickly herded the party into the Crown Hotel where they were to eat before going to the local cinema. Leaving Charles and the other boys briefly to their own devices in the hotel lounge, Green popped along to book the cinema seats.

Just as people climbed up at church windows to peer at the boy's parents when they were on their honeymoon, so other people now began to stare in at Charles through the windows of the hotel. Unnerved by this—'Absolutely fed up', as he expressed it in schoolboy fashion—he retreated into the next room. It happened to be the hotel's cocktail bar. He was immediately subject to more nudge-nudging and wink-winking on the part of those drinking there and, not unnaturally, became more nervously embarrassed than ever. Whether out of a sense of schoolboy bravado or because he felt in need of a psychological 'crutch' at that particular moment, Charles went to the bar and ordered himself a glass of cherry brandy. It was the only drink with which he was familiar at the time, having been given the occasional nip to keep the cold out when out shooting with his father. Nor at his age, and brought up in a family which does not go pubbing, could he be expected to know that Britain's somewhat archaic licensing laws prohibit the serving of drinks to anyone under the age of eighteen.

He paid for the drink—half-a-crown —and was in the act of sipping it when Donald Green returned from booking the cinema seats. 'What are you doing in here?' he immediately wanted to know.

Someone else witnessed the incident too, a journalist who Charles was later heard to refer to as 'that dreadful woman', and within twenty-four hours the story that the young Prince of Wales had broken the law by purchasing a drink on licensed premises was front-page news around the world.

In Britain, coupled with the fact that the name *Pinta** served as a link with the Milk Marketing Board's exhortation to 'drinka pinta milka day', it was perhaps taken for the trivial, amusing incident it really was. But in countries with no knowledge of Britain's quaint drinking laws it became blown up out of all proportion and the impression was given that the schoolboy prince had been indulging in some sort of boozy spree.

Nor, unfortunately, did things end there. Buckingham Palace, approached for an official comment, naturally contacted Donald Green. A misunderstanding over the telephone resulted in a flat royal denial of the whole business.

Back to the woman journalist. She stuck to her story. There were more tele-

*NAMED AFTER ONE OF CHRISTOPHER COLUMBUS' THREE SHIPS

phone calls between Buckingham Palace and Scotland. The earlier official denial was withdrawn, the original story was told all over again in a fresh form and a chastened Prince Charles returned to Gordonstoun to be disciplined by his headmaster.

He had earlier qualified for what was known at Gordonstoun as the Junior Training Plan, the first step up in the school's system of what the then headmaster, Mr F.R.G. Chew, described to us as 'turning out good citizens and bringing out qualities of leadership in boys who possess them'. Charles was naturally proud of this youthful achievement and when, as punishment, his Junior Training Plan was taken away and he had to set about qualifying for it all over again, he felt he was being unjustly treated. He was further hurt when Donald Green, to whom he had become attached, saw fit to resign his post soon after. Charles considered it all highly unfair. The memory of it was to rankle in his mind for years after and perhaps still does.

Nevertheless, he had learned another

important lesson in the way of royal life and thereafter was doubly careful not to do anything which might conceivably attract attention to himself. Other boys from Gordonstoun might occasionally go to the local 'caff'—Pete's—to drink Coke, play the jukebox and chat up the girls, but not Charles. Other boys might indulge in dormitory 'rags' after lights out, but not Charles. More than ever he was marked as being 'different', a boy alone.

However much his parents may have desired it, even at Gordonstoun he could not live an 'ordinary' boyhood and the strain told. There was an occasion when he went to Edinburgh to sing in St Giles' Cathedral with the school choir. As always, the photographers were lying in wait for him when he came out. Feeling sorry for him, the other boys grouped themselves around him and smuggled him unseen on to the school bus.

'They never leave me alone,' he confided in the boy in the next seat. 'I wonder sometimes if it's all worth it.'

Try as he would, he could never completely avoid publicity. Like some unseen old man of the sea, the threat of it sat always on his young shoulders. And sometimes the burden, through no fault of his own, would get out of control and take over...as when one of his school essays books did a vanishing act.

The story of the disappearing essay book found its way into the newspapers and inevitably grew with the telling. An American magazine came out with the theory that Charles had sold the essays himself to augment his pocket money. This brought a sharp official denial from Buckingham Palace. But that someone had sold the essay book to someone was undeniable. In fact it seems to have changed hands several times and at increasing prices which would have done credit to a piece of property speculation.

Scotland Yard came into the picture and appears to have handled its investigation in a rather heavy-handed way as though dealing with a breach of national security rather than the loss of a school essay book. However, heavy-handedness brought results and the book was finally recovered, but not before its contents had been photo-copied and translation rights sold to a German magazine.

Two of the published essays yielded clues to the Prince's schoolboy views (which have perhaps changed somewhat over the years since) on democracy—he deplored the tendency to 'vote for a certain party and not for individual people'—and on the press, which curiously enough, for all his own unhappy experiences, he was inclined to defend. While criticizing newspapers for the way in which they embarrassed some people by what they published, he was also at pains to point out that at the same time they 'protect people from the Government by letting them know what is going on, perhaps behind their backs in some cases'. Of the other two items published, one was hardly an essay while the other was not, in its original form, the boy's work. The hardly-an-essay one was his list of articles he would find most useful if cast away on a desert island, a perhaps predictable selection of tent, knife, rope and portable radio. The other was a précis of an extract from William Lecky's *History of England in the Eighteenth Century*.

Despite his loneliness there, Gordonstoun was undoubtedly good for Charles, as he has recognized himself over the years since. He has said, looking back on his schooldays, 'I think public school gives you a great deal of self-discipline, experience and responsibility, and it is the responsibility which is so worthwhile.'

Gordonstoun helped to toughen and mature him. His chubbiness evaporated even if his shyness lingered on. Conscientious if not brilliant, he toiled away dutifully at both lessons and games. He gained his O-levels in English language, English literature, history, French, Latin and later and with some difficulty mathematics. He learned first aid, tried his hand at pottery, went on an expedition to the Cairngorms, and, putting all these things together, qualified for both a 'bronze' and 'silver' in his father's Duke of Edinburgh Award Scheme.

But he was still, in many respects, a square peg in a scholastic round hole. Increasingly it was becoming clear that while there were many qualities in him waiting to be developed, they were not necessarily the qualities which distinguished Prince Philip, his father, and that Gordonstoun was not necessarily the best place to develop them.

Yet he could hardly be taken away from Gordonstoun at this comparatively late stage and sent elsewhere, at least in Britain. To do so would look distinctly odd, to say the least. But to send him to school for a time in one of the countries of the Commonwealth would not look in the least bit odd. That sorted out, it remained only to decide where. It was his father who suggested Australia. Philip has seen something of that country during his years as a naval officer and had liked it there.

Sir Robert Menzies, visiting the Royals at Balmoral that year, was asked what school he thought would be most suitable. He suggested Geelong Church of England Grammar School in Victoria. However, because of the danger that publicity could be as big in Australia as in Britain, that the Australian public might turn the schoolboy prince into what Sir Robert called 'a raree show', Charles went not to the main school, but to Timbertop, an educational outpost located some 116 miles from Melbourne where boys from the middle school combined academic studies with some experience of living rough in the Australian bush.

Timbertop, as Charles quickly found out, was no less rugged than Gordonstoun—indeed, he ranks it as 'rougher'—yet he loved it there. For two main reasons. One was an agreement with the newspapers over publicity. On the day of his arrival reporters and photographers were given almost the complete run of the place—on the clear understanding that thereafter they would leave him entirely alone. The agreement may not have been kept completely, but to a large extent it was observed.

The other reason was the very different attitude which the Australian boys at Timbertop adopted towards him. If he was not just another ordinary boy, and he could hardly be that, then neither was he someone on a very much loftier plane. If he was different, it was because he hailed from Britain—not because he was royal. There was none of the awe-struck reverence nor the obsequious genuflecting he had known at Gordonstoun. For the first time in his life the atmosphere around him was as near normal as it could hope to be and the day he walked in carrying the traditional English umbrella to be greeted by laughing shouts of 'Pommy bastard' he felt that the barriers were finally down.

If his academic studies were necessarily different—because he was working towards the A-levels in French and history he would be taking on his return to Britain while the other youngsters, mostly about two years his junior, were working towards their own Australian examinations—he joined wholeheartedly in the more rugged aspects of life at Timbertop. As always, some of the things which appeared in the newspapers were exaggerated and an article in the school magazine gives a more accurate, if less flamboyant, picture.

'Prince Charles is not treated as a typical boy. He is subordinate only to the masters and supervises the other boys. He only has to be up for breakfast at 7.30. He does not perform any menial tasks or sleep in the same quarters as the other boys. Prince Charles does, however, participate in things like chopping wood for the boilers and looking after the pigs and poultry.'

If he had his own sleeping quarters, he did eat with the other boys. He did go on long cross-country treks, humping his own camping gear and rations. He played some polo, did some fishing and tried his hand, not very successfully, at the Australian art of sheep shearing.

His own joking footnotes to all this are to be found in an article entitled 'Beatling Around The Bush' which he wrote later for the *Gordonstoun Record*. Of his first experience of wood-chopping he wrote: 'I could hardly see my hands for blisters.' On selecting a suitable camp site while on trek: 'You virtually have to inspect every inch of ground in case there are ants or other ghastly creatures. There is one species called bull ants which are three-quarters of an inch long or more and bite like mad.' Schoolwork, he added, could not 'be taken quite as seriously as in an ordinary school'.

The Queen Mother, making a royal tour of New Zealand and Australia, rearranged her schedule so that she could see her grandson at the end of his first term. They met in Canberra and Charles accompanied her on a tour of the Snowy Mountains. And this time there was no plea to intercede with his parents to let him leave the school. On the contrary, he was enjoying himself so much that he could tell his grandmother that he had already telephoned home for permission to stay on for another term.

4   Student*

Prince Charles has said several times, in different ways, that the period he spent at Timbertop proved to be one of the major turning points in his young life.

'Australia got me over my shyness.'

'I was able for the first time to look outwards.'

'More than any other experience, those years opened my eyes.'

But memory can play tricks even with royal memories. In fact, he was at Timbertop only some five months, not 'years'. And those five months did not entirely cure him of his inherited shyness. It was still there, and he still blushed rather freely, during the early months at Cambridge which lay ahead.

But it is undeniable that, in other respects, he had changed while at Timbertop—or, at very least, that a process

*APPENDIX II

of change had begun; undeniable that those months in Australia did something to him. It was not only that he looked bronzed and life-guardish when he joined his father and sister in Jamaica for the 1966 Commonwealth Games.* It was more than that; something inside him which showed outwardly in the way he held himself; the newly assured way he moved and the fresh spring in his step when walking. Gone was the hesitant schoolboy of Cheam and Gordonstoun with his hunched shoulders and shuffling feet, his place taken by a mature young man with shoulders braced, a ready grin and a sometimes slightly over-hearty handshake, much more relaxed and confident (or so it seemed) when it came to coping with the protocol niceties of public occasions. It was as though what had once unnerved him was now a challenge he was determined to master.

Charles himself has said that he can pinpoint the exact day—indeed, almost the exact minute—when his earlier apprehension of his public position was

*APPENDIX IV

exorcized.

He was on his way, one of a party of some thirty boys from Timbertop, for an educational visit to Papua New Guinea. As always, news of his coming travelled ahead of him and the inevitable crowd was waiting to greet him when his aircraft made a refuelling touch-down at Brisbane.

Charles has recalled that another member of the party (he has not said who) suggested that he should get out of the aircraft and show himself to the crowd. That was perhaps the last thing he would have done had he been left entirely to his own devices. Crowds, at that time, still bothered him. 'I had to be virtually kicked out of the plane,' he remembers. While this is perhaps a joking overstatement, clearly he was more of a pressed man than a volunteer.

However reluctantly, he finally left the aircraft. Then, as he walked towards the waiting crowd, 'something clicked inside me...From that moment I have never felt nervous in public.'

The metamorphosis which started at Timbertop was to be completed during his years at Trinity College, Cambridge. While Charles himself may think that Australia performed the entire personality conjuring trick, not everyone would agree. And it is the looker-on perhaps who sometimes sees more of the play. Lord Butler, Master of Trinity, for instance, remembers that Charles was still 'very boyish, somewhat immature and perhaps too susceptible to family influence' when he first went there. In his Lordship's view, it was the years at Trinity which 'really changed him; made him grow up'.

Timbertop or Trinity...we are inclined to think that both played an important part; that the personality change Prince Charles has undergone was a gradual process which had started even before he went to Timbertop, at Gordonstoun, and perhaps even before that, on the very first day he was jerked free of Nanny Lightbody's apron-strings and dispatched to Hill House. Timbertop undoubtedly played an extremely important part, serving as a sort of psychological couch on which Charles was to shed many of his inhibitions. So did Trinity.

So, later, did the Navy...and the process of change is perhaps even now not fully complete. With Charles not long married, it would be unusual if it was.

Following his spell in Australia, Charles returned to Gordonstoun for a further year to take his A-levels in French and history—he also followed in his father's footsteps by becoming Guardian (the equivalent to head boy in more orthodox schools)—before going to university.

The decision that he should go to university had already been taken at the time he celebrated his eighteenth birthday, that all-important constitutional landmark which separates the royal men from the boys. At eighteen, in the tragic event of anything happening to his mother, Charles could succeed to the throne without the necessity for his father to play the Regent. He would not only be King, but be able to act as King with no paternal interference. This being so, clearly his future education was now of too much importance to be left merely to the desires and decisions of his parents.

Such being the case, a small conference of the topmost brass was convened at Buckingham Palace. Charles, though the person most affected by whatever might be decided, was apparently not present. The Queen was, but did not join in the debate. She merely posed the question: What do we do with Charles when he finishes at Gordonstoun? Philip, as father, took the chair. Also present were the then prime minister, Harold Wilson (representing the State), the Archbishop of Canterbury (representing the Church); Earl Mountbatten of Burma (there not as a member of the family, but representing the Services); another Wilson—Sir Charles (chairman of the Committee of Vice-Chancellors); and the Dean of Windsor, Dr Robin Woods, who had previously prepared Charles for confirmation.

There was, it seems, some sort of half-hearted suggestion (as to who made it, your guess is as good as ours) that Charles should go to one of the new red-brick universities, but it does not seem to have been pushed very far. However, the general feeling was that somewhere more traditional would be more appropriate and Dr Woods was appointed as a sort of one-man sub-committee to come up with a specific recommendation.

Prince Philip is on record as saying that Charles 'wanted to go to university', though desire would seem to have followed decision. What Charles did want, for certain, was to feel that he was going to university as a matter of merit and not simply as a spot of royal privilege. Hence the return to Gordonstoun and the tackling of A-levels. He passed successfully and, indeed, was among only six per cent of the 4000 history candidates who gained a distinction in the special optional paper.

Despite this, there was, perhaps inevitably, a quota of jeers and jibes when it first became known that he was going to university. A group of sixth-formers at a grammar school in Suffolk who were themselves competing for places at university wrote to a newspaper accusing Charles of 'a blatant use of his royal prerogative'. The National Union of Students tabled a sarcastic motion expressing 'concern' for the 'hardship' his parents might experience if he did not receive a student grant. And even the National Union of Teachers, which should surely have been able to rise above the level of schoolboys and students, labelled him 'a royal border-liner'.

It all hit home and some of it stung. Those who dispense such jibes are perhaps inclined to forget that the Royals are also human beings, not stuffed dummies or waxwork figures; that they have feelings like the rest of us. Prince Philip said on one occasion that he had reached the stage in life when he could read about himself 'like some animal in the Zoo'. We doubt if that is completely true even in the case of Prince Philip, a more sensitive man than you might suspect, and certainly Charles, not quite eighteen at the time, had not then completed the emotional case-hardening which is part of royal growing-up and, indeed, perhaps never will.

Dr Woods, after cogitating the matter for a time, suggested Trinity College at Cambridge as being a suitable venue for the further development of Prince

Charles' academic qualities. One of his reasons for so doing was that the student body there contained a higher-than-usual proportion of grammar school boys. This, it was felt, would give the heir to the throne, if not exactly an opportunity of seeing how the other half lives, at least the possibility of mixing with it talking to it and obtaining some idea of what makes it tick.

If some people jeered at the idea of Charles going to university, there were others who hailed it as another bold royal experiment. In fact, it was not quite as revolutionary as all that. Other Royals had been to university in the past. Edward VII, great-great-grandfather of the present Prince of Wales, went to no fewer than three—Cambridge, Oxford and Edinburgh—though it does not seem to have done him much good. George V, as a young man, went to Magdalen at Oxford, while the Queen's father, King George VI, also went to Trinity.

So there was nothing very novel in the idea that the heir to the throne should go to university. But in Charles' case, two things were distinctly revolutionary. One was the fact that he would stay at university for the full degree course and take a degree in open competition with other undergraduates. None of his forebears had done that. The other innovation was the idea that he should live in, something his grandfather, King George VI, was certainly not permitted to do. The college authorities of the day had pressed for him to do so, but his parents, George V and straight-backed Queen Mary with her perhaps rather lofty ideas of what was royally fit and proper, would not hear of it. Instead, a house was rented for him some distance from the college and, in consequence, he had little opportunity for mixing with other, less regal undergraduates.

The news that Charles was going to Trinity seems to have sent the college authorities into the customary state of tizzy which precedes a royal visit and there was the inevitable spate of spit-and-polish ahead of his arrival. Indeed, some of what was done may even have been by royal request. The impression is often given that the Royals long for nothing so much as to be treated as ordinary people, and perhaps sometimes they do, though if you are going to regard and treat them as ordinary then there would seem to be little point in having them at all. In any event, it depends of course on what you mean by 'ordinary'. What is regarded as ordinary by a royal prince or princess might well seem a lot less ordinary to those of us who really are ordinary.

Be that as it may, there was to be no question of freshman Charles charging across New Court each morning, towel in one hand, sponge bag and shaving kit in the other, to take his turn with other undergraduates in using the communal baths. Instead, rooms in one of the turrets which give New Court something of the atmosphere of a medieval fortress were altered and redecorated to provide him not only with a study and bedroom, but also with his own private bathroom and gyp room (or kitchenette). Later, when he became a third year student, he had rooms in Great Court.

Nor was a private bathroom the only privilege accorded to him in his freshman year. As a freshman, he was not permitted by the rules to keep a car within the university precincts. The problem was neatly overcome by garaging his red M.G., with its leather-covered steering wheel and throaty bull horn, just outside the limits. When he had need of it, his detective would run him over in a Land Rover to collect it. The college authorities may not have been entirely deceived, but they did nothing to close the legal loophole through which Charles occasionally drove his M.G.

His arrival at Trinity turned itself into a combination of royal occasion and pop-star welcome. As usual, he saw the funny side of the situation and was to joke in an article he wrote later about how he had arrived at Trinity 'wedged in a mini'. If this particular form of transport was specially selected in an attempt to underline the 'ordinariness' of his undergraduate image, it does not seem to have been his own idea, judging from the fact that he described it as 'a form of travel not normally employed when there are people to meet upon disembarkation'.

Charles squeezed out of his mini to be almost mobbed by a cheering, squealing mob of mini-skirted girls who pursued him enthusiastically as he walked towards the gateway of the college where Lord Butler was waiting to greet him.

Someone in the crowd called out, 'Good luck.'

'I'll need it,' Charles called back.

The girls continued to mob him and he was rescued only when, as he wrote in the article, 'several burly bowler-hatted gentlemen proceeded to drag shut those magnificent wooden gates to prevent the crowd following in'. It was, he recalled, 'rather like a scene from the French Revolution'.

Charles has long been, and still is, particularly fascinated by pre-history. His interest in the subject was first aroused when he was at Gordonstoun and became one of the group of boys there who set to work to excavate a cave which, rightly or wrongly, they judged had once been used as a cliff-face dwelling. Interest had been further stimulated, while in Australia, by the trip he made from Timbertop to Papua New Guinea and the glimpses he had there of a primitive people still practising the arts and crafts handed down through countless generations. It was perhaps no more than was to be expected that at Trinity he should decide to read what undergraduates know as 'ark and anth' and is listed in the syllabus as 'archaeology and anthropology'.

Prince Philip has been known to boast of himself as 'one of those stupid bums who never went to university', adding as a footnote, 'And I don't think it's done me any harm.' Charles, by the time he was twenty, could equally describe himself as 'one of those stupid bums who went to university', adding, with perhaps the gentlest of digs at dad, 'And I think it's helped me.'

The father who never went to university and the son who did have several important qualities in common. Or perhaps they are all facets of the same outstanding quality. Both have a tremendous aptitude for hard work, are doers rather than watchers on the stage of life, dislike nothing so much as merely sitting round and twiddling their thumbs but must always be up and doing. Charles, earlier on, may have watched too much television when he would have been better employed reading worthwhile books, but at Trinity he more than made up for it. Conscientiously—and perhaps conscious of the fact that he is an academic plodder rather than an intellectual genius—he crammed more than most into the average day, attending more lectures than most of the other students, turning out more essays.

In addition to attending lectures and turning out essays, he continued the 'cello-playing he had started at Gordonstoun and played with the college orchestra, he joined an amateur acting group called the Dryden Society and took part in a number of stage productions,* and even found time, to pose for a group photograph of what might be termed 'the Class of '69'.

He went on a number of archaeological 'digs' with mixed groups of other ark and anth students. In the course of one such expedition the group inadvertently trespassed on private land and found themselves intercepted by an irate

*CHAPTER 5

144

landowner who, according to another member of the party, was already in the process of 'bawling us out' when he recognized Prince Charles. His manner changed immediately and he became 'quite fawning'. Embarrassed far more by such obsequiousness than ever he had been by the original bawling-out, Charles blushed beetroot red and walked hurriedly away.

He tried hard, and with a considerable degree of success, to melt into the university background. The previous Prince of Wales, when he was at university, had been conspicuous for his fur-collared coat. Charles, by contrast, was often seen around in baggy corduroy trousers and a tweed jacket with leather-patched elbows, walking or cycling to lectures. He toured the stalls in the local market, had an occasional drink in a local pub and shopped in the local chain stores. One such shopping expedition revealed that however little he had known about money when he first went to Hill House, he had more than caught up over the years since. He bought himself an umbrella and carefully counted his change before moving on.

'Excuse me,' he said to the nervous and excited assistant who had served him, 'but have you given me enough?'

She hadn't. He was £1 short.

If one of the reasons for picking Trinity had been the expectation that Charles might chum up with a few former grammar school boys, it cannot be said in all honesty that this part of the experiment was a success. Much has been made of his acquaintanceship—it hardly acquired the depths of friendship—with Hywell Jones, a young Welsh left-winger reading economics and president of the Trinity Students' Union and the fact that they were still in touch with each other some years later. But this was simply the exception which proved the rule. While no one may have stood to attention when Charles walked into a lecture room, as they did for his great-great-grandfather, the rule at Trinity, as at Gordonstoun, was that there was a gulf separating royalty from the common man which it was almost impossible to bridge from either side.

In the case of Hywell Jones, such

146

bridging as was achieved seems to have been done mainly by Charles. Like others before and since, Jones, initially, was concerned that no one—least of all Charles himself—should suspect him of sucking up. 'I didn't want him to think I was talking to him just because he was the Prince of Wales,' he explained. And certainly he had no intention of cashing in on the acquaintanceship, as he quickly showed when approached by a newspaper to write a series of articles entitled 'My Friend Prince Charles'. The newspaper was prepared to pay substantially, but Jones rejected the offer out of hand.

In his early days at least, Charles himself was almost as backward in coming forward, though this was not for want of trying. He tried, for instance, having his meals in hall with the other undergraduates. But despite the fresh confidence he felt he had acquired in Australia, he quickly found it too much of an ordeal. 'I'm still a bit shy, but I'm working on it,' he was to say around this time and, for once, he was not altogether joking. Instead of eating in hall, he stayed in his rooms at mealtimes, making his own toast and coffee for breakfast and having his other meals sent up to him.

Bit by bit, however, he did manage to establish some sort of relationship with some of the other students either because, like Hywell Jones, they lived on the same 'stair' as he did or went to the same lectures or were fellow-members of the Dryden Society. From time to time he would invite a bunch of them up to his room to drink coffee, munch shortbread, listen to folk music and traditional jazz played on the stereo set which was a birthday present from his father, and generally 'chew the fat', as the saying goes. If the others, in the course of such 'bull' sessions, were concerned to set the world to rights, Charles was equally concerned not to say anything that might be construed as being even remotely controversial. He had not the slightest desire for a repeat performance of the cherry brandy incident at Gordonstoun, with newspaper headlines perhaps proclaiming that the Prince of Wales was for or against Welsh Nationalism, coloured immigration or what-have-you. But while carefully not expressing an opinion himself on such topics, he became near-expert at asking the sort of subtle questions which would keep the rest arguing. However, he did pipe up and say his piece the day another student expressed the view that Britain's monarchs had always been a bunch of intellectual philistines. Not so, retorted Charles, and proceeded to prove his case with an argument that went all the way back to King James I and his *Counterblast To Tobacco* treatise.

He made a number of other attempts to get on terms with his fellow-students, even to the extent of going along to one or two student parties (though he was careful to avoid the sort of party where cheap wine is served in paper cups and the lights are turned down for couples to pair off in darkened corners). But, in the main, he found such attempts heavy going, sometimes because 'suckers'—his own word—of either sex would thrust themselves at him and sometimes because he felt his presence was having a dampening effect upon the proceedings.

'I've been here over an hour and they

haven't even put the record-player on yet,' he confided in a fellow-student at one party. 'I'm sure I'm putting a damper on things. I think I'd better go so that they can start enjoying themselves.'

His companion may have protested politely that the rest *were* enjoying themselves, but Charles knew better. And he left.

'He tried very hard to get the others to accept him as just an ordinary student,' an ex-Trinity man recalls. 'He really worked at it. But you couldn't say that he succeeded. My own view is that sometimes he worked *too* hard at it, talking too much with everyone else standing around him more or less tongue-tied. Then a sort of tension would set in.'

Just as he had given up going along to hall for his meals, so Charles, in time, was to give up most of his other efforts at mixing at all levels, though never the Dryden Society which he enjoyed for its own sake. He did make friends, but they were hardly ex-grammar school boys. On the contrary, they were what the ex-grammar school boys knew as 'the huntin' fishin' and shootin' set', a small, select coterie of undergraduates with hyphenated names, Old Etonian backgrounds or titled fathers.

A group of them, including Charles, formed themselves into a small dining circle known as the Wapiti Club. But even among this small, select group, Charles was always conscious of his position and careful to act accordingly. One or two others might sometimes indulge too freely. He did not. Others might talk freely and volubly. He did not; could not. Always he must steer clear of such controversial issues as religion, politics and race. On the other hand, it was only human nature that he should not wish to be considered a spoilsport. So when the others, one night after wining and dining, embarked on a slalom-type bicycle race in and out of the cloisters of Nevile's Court, he joined in. The late-night racket they kicked up was so great that it brought Dr Seal, the Director of Studies, out of his residence with a stern injunction that if they did not 'desist' at once he would summon the proctor.

His father, sister and grandmother all visited Charles in his rooms at Trinity at varying times. So did his mother, though not until he had been there some eighteen months and she had good excuse for dropping in on him. She was in Cambridge for the fiftieth anniversary of the National Institute of Agricultural Botany and took advantage of the fact to join her son for a lunch of mushroom soup followed by fried chicken.

More than anything, Charles was anxious that his fellow-students should not regard him as some sort of royal stuffed shirt or spoilsport. 'I often feel that the whole fun of university life is breaking the rules,' he said on one occasion. 'Half the fun at Cambridge is to climb in at all hours of the night.' In fact, Charles himself broke very few rules during his spell at Trinity, though he did participate in one or two small and harmless student rags which, fortunately for him, attracted far less attention from the press than the cherry brandy incident of his Gordonstoun days.

However, the newspapers were quick to reprint extracts from a lighthearted article he wrote for the student magazine *Varsity* in which he lamented jokingly over the difficulty he was experiencing in accustoming himself to the 'grinding note' the local dustcart made on its early-morning rounds, to the 'head-splitting clang' of dustbins emptied and the 'monotonous jovial dustman's refrain of "O Come All Ye Faithful".'

Joking though his comments so obviously were, the emptying of the dustbins in his vicinity was promptly put back from seven to nine in the morning to avoid disturbing his slumbers and the singing dustman, Frank Clarke, who described himself as 'a bit of a Harry Secombe' (though his wife was apparently inclined to think of him 'more as an Al Jolson') was offered a contract by an enterprising recording company. The article also led to Charles himself being offered a contract, though not to sing. A national newspaper announced itself prepared to pay him £10,000 a year if he cared to turn out the occasional article for publication. Charles, conscious of the fact that the newspaper was more anxious to acquire a princely by-line than whatever literary talent he might have, decided not to accept.

Having passed Part I of his tripos, he moved on to a study of more modern history. But more and more his studies were interrupted by the need to perform royal chores.* The affairs of the Duchy of Cornwall also took up an increasing amount of his time and added to this was the necessity to start learning Welsh with the aid of some Welsh-language records in preparation for his investiture as Prince of Wales. Yet he still found time for a radio interview with Jack de Manio designed to bolster the princely image ahead of the investiture, to embark on a course of flying lessons and to take part in a student debate around the question of whether mankind's technological advance posed a threat to the individuality of man.

Charles felt that it did and, in the course of the debate, questioned the value and validity of the Anglo-French supersonic wonder-plane, Concorde. 'If it is going to pollute with noise, if it is going to knock down churches and shatter priceless windows, as some say it

*CHAPTER 6

will, is it really what we want?' he queried.

There is an echo in this of some of the more outspoken remarks his father has made from time to time, even if Philip, speaking on the same topic a few years later, was to take a contrary view over Concorde. But coming from the son, the sort of remark which has all too often found the father in hot water, attracted a good deal less criticism.

To maintain the fiction that the Welsh were really getting a prince of their own, it was decided that Charles should transfer from Trinity to the University College of Aberystwyth ahead of his investiture as Prince of Wales.* Politically desirable though this move may have been, the wonder is that it was not academically disastrous. Charles himself, though appreciating the motive behind this change of venue, was far from happy at being uprooted from Trinity just as he was feeling that he had really begun to settle in.

At Aberystwyth, as so often before

*CHAPTER 6.

155

and since, he was to find himself with divided loyalties. This time it was the necessity to be both student and prince at one and the same time. As prince, he found himself taking a cram course in the Welsh language. As student, he did his best to continue reading for his Cambridge degree. Almost inevitably his degree studies suffered and later he was to take an eight-week course in speed-reading to enable him to catch up.

Constant interruptions to his normal academic curriculum, the need to do so many other things at the same time, would have made life difficult for even the most brilliant student. And Charles has never pretended to be brilliant. To him, learning has never come easy and his degree course at Trinity was no exception. Such academic success as he has achieved has been the result of strict self-discipline, application and concentration, with perhaps also a little help from the unusually inquiring nature which he seems to have inherited from his father. Both father and son will take nothing on trust. To convince them of anything requires not only the facts but the reasoning behind the facts. Even then, the reasoning does not always pass without argument. Philip, when he was younger, had a considerable reputation for arguing with his naval instructors. 'He would argue so much,' remembers a man who was once on the same course with him, 'that it was sometimes hard to know who was supposed to be giving the lecture, the instructor or Philip.' Charles, in university days, may not have taken over from his tutors to quite that extent, but he would certainly argue a point if he was not entirely convinced.

But hard work was the principal ingredient. Following research in the college's Wren-designed library, the light —if not the oil—often burned late in his rooms as, at the peak of his studies, he churned out sometimes as many as three essays a week though only one was required of him. And when, in June 1970, his name—*Wales, HRH Prince of*—was sandwiched between those of Vaux J.E.G. and Walker J.N.G. in the list of results, it would be fair to say that he had earned his degree, Bachelor of Arts (Cantab.) the hard way.

5 Entertainer

While Charles toiled diligently and conscientiously during his years at Cambridge, he was also conscious of the fact
that all work and no play could make
Charles, equally with Jack, a dull fellow.
To avoid any such fate, he took full advantage of the many opportunities which
university life afforded him in non-aca-
demic directions. He played cello, played
polo*, went out with one or two girls and
grabbed wholeheartedly at the chance of
making a 'legitimate fool' of himself by
appearing on stage in a whole range of
lunatic roles. Indeed, it is perhaps not
stretching things too far to hazard the
opinion that it was his amateur stage
appearances at Cambridge which helped
him finally to shed those inhibitions
which still lingered from the cosseted
days of childhood.

*CHAPTER 7

Charles has perhaps always been something of a 'ham,' a would-be actor with a talent for mimicry (which his mother also has) and a gift for comic inventiveness. Had he been born in more humble circumstances, one can visualize him leaving school to join a third-rate repertory company, touring the country, living in theatrical digs, tackling all sorts of stage jobs from scrounging properties for *The Boy Friend* to playing the third grave-digger in *Hamlet,* then working his way up the ladder of revue, farce and light comedy until he made Broadway and the West End. Because he is who he is, we will never see him on the West End stage, but more and more in the years ahead we can expect to see him on television, a field in which he has already achieved something of a reputation as an interviewer and commentator if not actor.

As with so many children, dressing-up games were among his favourites in childhood. He was perhaps more fortunate than most children in that his playthings included a big box of dressing-up clothes, containing everything from an Indian head-dress his parents brought back from a royal tour of Canada to a miniature knight's outfit which was one of his early Christmas presents. Inevitably, childhood dressing-up games were conditioned by the pattern of his environment and background. 'Coronations' became a favourite game following his visit to Westminster Abbey to watch part of his mother's coronation ceremony. Charles, in a miniature cloak, would play the king while Anne, with a borrowed tablecloth draped round her shoulders, was his queen. And it was presumably a glimpse of a royal investiture from the balcony of the palace ballroom which caused him to have two of his mother's footmen kneel before him while he 'knighted' them with a toy sword. Later he revelled in games of charades, a favourite party game with the Royal Family ever since Queen Alexandra's day.

His first opportunity to appear on stage came while he was a schoolboy at Cheam. With his parents in the audience, he joined in the singing of some sea shanties and also took part in a skit entitled *Ten Little Cheam Boys*. A spot of more serious acting came his way, though still at the schoolboy level, with the presentation of a play called *The Last Baron* which had been written by David Munir, one of the masters. Initially, Charles was merely one of the understudies. Then the boy given the role of the Duke of Gloucester who became King Richard III had to withdraw from the part and Charles stepped into the breach.

The play was presented on an improvised stage in the school hall on 19th February 1960, by coincidence the same day on which Prince Andrew was born. For this reason, the Queen was unable to witness her eleven-year-old son's acting début, which was perhaps as well, though she would doubtless have done nothing more than a smile at the spectacle of her youthful heir mouthing such lines as 'Soon may I ascend the throne' which would have been considered highly treasonable in less enlightened times. According to the school magazine, Charles revealed 'a good voice and excellent elocution' in a role which 'well conveyed the ambition and bitterness of the twisted hunchback'.

If such ability as Charles has shown as an actor stems mainly from his mother, who took part in a number of amateur pantomimes staged at Windsor Castle during the war years, he also has other artistic qualities which have presumably come down to him from his father. Philip's artistic ability has perhaps been overshadowed over the years by his more newsworthy athletic image, but his stubby fingers have proved themselves capable of many other things besides handling a gun and swinging a polo mallet. At varying times he has constructed an excellent scale model of Balmoral Castle, designed a rose garden for Windsor, a bracelet for his wife and an ornamental collar as a greyhound racing trophy, taken wild-life photographs good enough for reproduction and executed some passable oil paintings, one of which the Queen liked sufficiently to hang in their private quarters at Windsor.

We have Mabel Anderson's word for it that Charles was 'all fingers and thumbs' in childhood—Anne was the clever one—but a childish talent for drawing and painting was revealed when he went to Hill House day school. He still enjoys painting, though the opportunities to indulge in it have become fewer with the years, and has executed the occasional water colour in recent years. Schooldays also turned his hands into something more than fingers and thumbs. At Cheam he made a small table for Anne and gave it to her as a birthday present. He made a pen-stand for Miss Peebles, a tea-tray for Mabel Anderson and a book-rack for his mother. At Gordonstoun he tried his hand at carpentry, metalwork and pottery, several examples of his pottery being considered of sufficient standard to merit display in the school's arts and crafts exhibition one year.

A love of music and a passable singing voice also emerged during his school years. At Gordonstoun he sang with the school choir and played with the school orchestra. He had first learned the piano at home in childhood and piano lessons continued at Cheam. But the piano, he soon came to realize, was not really his instrument. At Gordonstoun he switched to the trumpet, playing officially with the school orchestra and unofficially in a small beat group some of the boys organized among themselves, though honesty compels us also to record that his practice sessions were not always popular with his school-fellows or some of the masters.

Charles would be the first to admit the truth of this. In fact, several times, in interviews, he had laughed himself at the recollections of playing trumpet with the school orchestra.

'We made an awful noise in the back row. I can hear the music teacher now. We'd all be playing away, making a hell of a din, and suddenly she couldn't stand it any longer. She would put down her violin and we'd all stop and she'd shout—she had a heavy German accent and somehow that made her sound more agonized—"Ach, ze trumpet. I cannot stand ze trumpet, Stawp ze trumpet".'

It was soon clear that he was not going to be another Louis Armstrong. Nevertheless, as persevering as always, he continued with the trumpet until he finally realized, as he has admitted himself, that his playing was getting on his own nerves quite as much as on those of other people.

His decision to give up the trumpet was also reinforced by hearing cellist Jacqueline du Pré and her husband, Daniel Barenboim, in a concert at Festival Hall. 'I'd never heard sounds like it,' he has recalled and nothing would satisfy him but he must try to emulate them. So it was over to the cello. His first tutor, Ella Taylor, was quoted as saying that he played 'brilliantly for someone learning for such a short time'. Charles, though he played the instrument in a recital in St Giles' Cathedral, Edinburgh, would not agree.

Gordonstoun also afforded him further opportunities for acting. He sang in the chorus of a school production of Gilbert and Sullivan's *Patience,* played the part of the Duke of Exeter in Shakespeare's *Henry V* and, at the age of seventeen, found himself with the title role in *Macbeth*. He took his acting, as he takes most things in life, with considerable seriousness. Ahead of *Macbeth* he acquired the recordings of Sir Laurence Olivier and played them over and over again to help improve his performance. He grew his hair long enough to avoid the necessity for wearing a wig, but could hardly, while still at school, cultivate the necessary beard. An artificial one served him in good stead and his parents, making an overnight journey from London to see the play, agreed with Gordonstoun's headmaster, Mr Chew, that their son acquitted himself 'excellently' in the demanding role.

But Gordonstoun, with the possible exception of the part of the Pirate King in a subsequent production of *The Pirates of Penzance,* gave him little opportunity to 'play the fool'. This had to wait upon Cambridge where he applied to join the Dryden Society. He was auditioned and accepted. His first stage appearance at Cambridge was as the camp padre in the Joe Orton comedy. *Erpingham Camp.* Wearing a clerical dog-collar borrowed from the Rev. Harry Williams, Dean of Trinity Chapel, the heir to the throne underwent the

166

indignity of having a custard pie slapped in his face, an action which would have horrified his great-great-great-grandmother, Queen Victoria, had she been alive to witness it, or even his great-grandmother, Queen Mary. That it did not unduly perturb either his mother or his grandmother shows the extent to which royal attitudes and outlooks have changed in recent years.

Worse—at least, from the dead Queen Victoria's point of view—was to follow. In a two-hour collection of under-graduate sketches lumped together under the punny title of *Revu-lution,* the dead Queen's great-great-great-grandson pranced about the stage in a whole variety of mickey-taking roles from a Victorian lecher to a dustman squatting in a dustbin, from a Beatle-wigged cello player to the Duke of Wellington winning the Battle of Waterloo.

Some of his roles followed so quickly upon one another that there was no time to nip up to the upstairs dressing-room for a change of costume. With a further disregard for royal dignity, Charles changed at the side of the stage. To his roles on stage he brought his talent for mimicry and a range of improbable voices made famous in the Goon Shows by Harry Secombe, Peter Sellers, Spike Milligan and Michael Bentine.

Charles has long been an admirer of the Goons and still is. He listened avidly to the repeats of their shows when they were broadcast a few years back, has a collection of their recordings and a tie dotted with decorative whales was given to him by Harry Secombe.

Secombe was wearing the tie when the two of them, prince and comedian, met on one occasion. Charles was quick to spot the decorative whales.

'I ought to be wearing that,' he joked. 'After all, I'm Prince of W(h)ales.'

Secombe promptly whipped it off and gave it to him.

Charles was duly grateful, as he subsequently proved when he was invited by *Punch* to review Secombe's book *Twice Brightly*. As might be expected from so ardent an admirer, it was hardly a critical review and Secombe later thanked him with a ballad which ended:

And lastly for our Royal guest,
A cheer from my wheezy chest;
Forgive my tendency to grovel
But he's just reviewed my latest novel.

As might be expected, the show *Revulution* was full of undergraduate 'in' jokes and not short on *double entendre*. The Prince's cello-playing pop star, just out of clink for smoking chicory, was described as 'the biggest plucker in the business'. As Sir Cummerband Overspill, the Victorian lecher, he marched off-stage with a pretty gipsy girl while delivering himself of the exit line: 'I like giving myself heirs'. As the Duke of Wellington, receiving the news that the French had fled from Waterloo, he sneered, 'Thank God. They've made a hell of a mess of the playing fields.'

As a singing dustman, he was, of course, taking a dig at himself, the joke deriving from the article he had written for *Varsity* complaining that the clanging of dustbins and the singing of dustman Frank Clarke woke him too early in the morning. 'What abart my £5?' he demanded as he squatted in his dustbin on stage while being interviewed by the press.

Whatever Queen Victoria might have thought about a descendant of hers behaving in so unseemly a fashion, the latter-day Royals had no such doubts. Prince Philip, Princess Anne and Princess Alexandra all went to see the show. Thanks to its princely 'star', it played to capacity houses throughout its brief four-night run and a Frenchman who telephoned from Paris after reading about it in the papers, with plans for bringing over a party of 200 people, found himself out of luck.

For his part, Charles thoroughly enjoyed himself in his role as amateur actor even if, in the words of a fellow-member of the Dryden Society, he was 'not quite as good an actor as the papers seem to think'. Never mind; the play's the thing. 'It's great fun,' Charles said, enthusiastically. 'I love doing it.' It was also perhaps, a form of psychological safety valve. 'It helps to keep me sane,' he confided in a friend. It may not have been a literal truth, but it was not necessarily a joke either.

The year following *Revu-lution*
Charles was again on stage with the
Dryden Society. The show had another
punny title—*Quiet Flows The Don*—and
the recipe was much the same mixture of
undergraduate humour and sexy
innuendo as before. In some ways, it was
almost a one-man show. There were
some thirty sketches in it and Charles
appeared in twenty-five of them, notably
as a weather forecaster (in gasmask and
frogman's flippers) announcing, between
blowing bubbles, that 'By morning
promiscuity will be widespread' and as
an expert in fourteenth-century Bong
Dynasty bidets who, confronted with the
task of identifying a set of bagpipes in an
antiques quiz-show, proclaimed them to
be 'an indigenous northern reptile with
stuffed tentacles'.

It was almost, though not quite, his
last stage appearance. There was to be in
after-years a gala performance at the
Royal Opera House when he disappeared
from his box...to re-appear on stage in
buccaneer garb during a send-up of *The
Pirates of Penzance*. But that was all.
However, there have been any number of

171

television appearances—as interviewer in a programme about the Welsh countryside; as commentator for a television tour of Canterbury Cathedral, for which he also wrote part of the script; a discussion on George III with Alistair Cooke; as interviewee on the occasion of his betrothal to Lady Diana Spencer.

His frenzied cello-plucking in *Revulution* was far from being the limit of his musical endeavours during his years at Trinity. He played in the college orchestra and took part in a concert in Trinity Chapel which included Mozart's *Magic Flute* overture, Beethoven's Fifth Symphony and Weber's bassoon concerto. He remembers it as 'a wonderful experience'.

At that time he was practising the cello assiduously, though never good at reading music, but other things—studying and royal duties—were later to curtail the amount of time available for music practice. Sometimes it was late at night before he could get round to practising, as happened the time a bunch of students spotted a light at his window. The episode of the singing dustman fresh in mind, they thought it would be a great lark to disturb Charles and then apologize profusely for doing so. So up the stairs they trooped to hammer on his door. However, this rather juvenile joke fell flat when Charles, answering the knocking, immediately proceeded to apologize himself: 'I hope my practising wasn't disturbing you.'

Despite his brief flirtation with the improvised beat group at Gordonstoun, Prince Charles' musical tastes have always been more classical than popular. With the exception of what he considered to be one or two of the more musical professional groups such as the Beatles— 'The Beatles sang splendid music; wrote great music'—and the Seekers, he was never really a teenage pop fan. Jazz he enjoys, though he admits to being 'no connoisseur'. But his real love is classical music. 'I find the more I listen to classical works, the more I get out of them.' Bach, Mozart and Beethoven are among his favourite composers. And there is a passage in *L'Enfance du Christ,* an oratorio by Hector Berlioz, which he has found can move him to tears. He first heard it while listening to one of the BBC's 'These You Have Loved' programmes.

'I thought I must get it. I play it now often. There is a certain passage in it which is so moving I'm reduced to tears.'

He enjoys both melody and rhythm. For this reason, he is 'not mad keen' on much modern music. 'A good deal of it is tuneless as far as I am concerned.'

He enjoys opera-going and is disappointed that his polo-playing seems to get so much more publicity. But opera-going did come in for publicity, though perhaps for the wrong reasons, when he went to Covent Garden in 1976 to see a new production of *L'Elisir d'Amour*. He was pictured in the papers accepting a flagon of 'love potion'—it was actually cheap Bordeaux wine—from Sir Geraint Evans who sang the role of the quack doctor in the production.

In an attempt to refute the 'philistine' label which is sometimes attached to his family, Charles has cited his mother's knowledgeable interest in both music and art—'She has immense taste,' he has said —and his father's oil painting. He him-

174

self is certainly a long way from being an intellectual philistine. We have his mother's word for it that there was a time when he would sit glued to the television screen instead of reading worthwhile books, as she would have preferred. That, of course, was before he went to Trinity and acquired the reading habit. Today he is not only a serious reader but has proved himself to be as adept with the pen as with the ornamental sword. His review of Harry Secombe's novel was only one of a number of literary efforts in recent years. There has been a best-selling children's book. There have been television scripts, a preface for a book of the Goon Shows, another for a book on wildlife, an article on his under-ice diving exploit for the magazine of the British Sub-Aqua Club when he was president, to say nothing of the lyrics of a witty ditty which were perhaps a shade too sophisticated for the Top Twenty even if they had been published commercially.* There was also a foreword for John Brooke's biography of George III.

*APPENDIX VI

Charles has a particularly soft spot for the great-great-great-great-great-grandfather in whose reign the American colonies gained their independence. But Charles is less concerned with the loss of America—it was bound to have happened sooner or later, he says—than with the fact that George III founded the Royal Academy, established the Royal Botanical Gardens at Kew and was an all-round patron of science, music and the arts, painting in particular.

'Most of the Royal Collection, or a lot of it, is the result of George III's acquisition and taste,' he told Alistair Cooke in the course of a conversation piece about this 'Much Maligned Monarch' which was televised in April 1976.

His great-great-great-great-great-grandfather, he said on another occasion, was a king whose style he would very much like to follow himself.

It was during his stint at the Royal Naval College, Greenwich, towards the tail-end of 1975, that Charles had lunch with Kenneth Pearson of the *Sunday Times*. Pearson was arranging the '1776' Exhibition to be held at the National

Maritime Museum the following year to mark the American Bicentennial. One of the exhibits was to be a tableau, complete with recorded dialogue, of the scene when John Adams, the former rebel who became America's first ambassador to Britain, presented his credentials to George III in the King's Closet at St James's Palace. Charles was enthusiastic. So much so that the Queen, listening to the recording when she opened the exhibition in the spring of 1976, could not resist a smiling reference to an 'agreeably familiar' voice.

Familiar indeed. For the voice which repeated the words of George III on the occasion of that historic meeting with Adams—'I wish you, sir, to believe, and that it may be understood in America, that I have done nothing in the late contest but what I thought myself indispensably bound to do by the duty I owed my people...I was the last to consent to the separation; but the separation having been made, and having become inevitable, I have always said, as I say now, that I would be the first to meet the friendship of the United States as an independent Power'—was that of Prince Charles, who made the recording at Buckingham Palace a few weeks after he lunched with Pearson.

The words of Adams, incidentally, were spoken by Elliot Richardson, former US ambassador to Britain and subsequently Secretary for Commerce in Washington.

In Charles' view, as he made clear in his television appearance with Alistair Cooke, George III is a much-misunderstood monarch whom history has settled upon as an easy target in its search for someone to blame for the loss of the American colonies.

'Generally speaking,' said Charles, 'the view that is particularly prevalent in schools is that George III was the mad king who lost the American colonies. That is all people seem to know about him...I do feel that it's very unfortunate if one is misunderstood in history. I personally would hate to be misunderstood... I should hate what happened in politics —what happened in an international sense—should mask him as a person, a human being, someone who was a great

178

patron of the arts, a great family man, and someone who was enormously loved and respected and appreciated in this country.'

He did not accept that his great-great-great-great-great-grandfather was mad. 'How do you define madness?' he asked Alistair Cooke. 'I would not say that George III was mad. He was not manic-depressive. He was not schizophrenic...I think it's been fairly conclusively proved that he suffered from a metabolic condition (porphyria) which affected the blood and which then affected to a certain extent his mind. He had hallucinations more than manic attacks.'

He was, he said, 'determined to clear his name'.

6 Apprentice

Those who would become doctors or nurses, lawyers or architects, even carpenters or plasterers, must first undergo a proper, and usually lengthy, period of tuition, training, apprenticeship. Not so those destined for future monarchy. In one sense—in the sense of sitting in a classroom or lecture hall listening to someone propound a list of royal duties and responsibilities—Prince Charles has never had a lesson in his life. In another sense, however, he has been trained for his present and future roles almost since birth. He has learned, as he has phrased it himself, 'the way a monkey learns—watching its parents'.

Training of a sort began before he was of an age even to take his parents as models. He was hardly more than five weeks old when we stood on the platform at Wolferton station, long since axed as part of the railway run-down, to watch the Royals arrive on their way to Sand-ringham for the Christmas of 1948. The royal train pulled in, they were greeted by the stationmaster, the divisional police chief and sundry other local bigwigs, then moved out into the station yard and climbed into the waiting cars. As the cars moved off Nanny Lightbody, who was carrying Charles, took his baby hand in hers and waved it at the small group of village folk and local journalists who had gathered to witness the royal arrival.

Even with a memory remarkable enough to remember being pushed around in his pram, it is unlikely that he can now remember anything of that frosty December evening at Wolferton. But there are other instances of childhood training which he will perhaps recall...like 'inspecting' the crew of the royal yacht *Britannia* when he first went aboard it at the age of five; shaking hands with members of the local recep-tion committee on another trip to Sandringham at around the same age. Wolferton station, that year, had been festively decorated with coloured bal-loons and the boy Charles could not keep his eyes from straying to them even as Prince Charles went through the hand-shaking routine. 'May I have a balloon, please?' he asked as soon as the red-carpet formalities were over.

His mother, by then, was already Queen and he was Duke of Cornwall though not yet Prince of Wales. He was just turned three at the time of his grand-father's death and, like any other small boy of the same age, was cushioned as much as possible from the trauma of the occasion. His mother was again away at the time, though not by her own wish. She was in Kenya, a halfway stop-over on the long haul to Australia and New Zealand where she was to carry out a royal tour as the deputy of her sick father. Charles and Anne, then a fluffy-topped toddler not yet eighteen months old, were staying with their grandparents at Sandringham. The dying King doted on his small grandchildren and it was his custom to sit with them each evening while they ate their supper, to talk with them and then to say prayers with Charles—Anne was not yet old enough to understand the significance of prayers

—when the boy went to bed. Then came the evening when there was no grandfather to sit with them at supper-time. Anne, still little more than a baby, may not have noticed his absence. But Charles did. 'Where is Grandpapa?' he wanted to know. No one could bring themselves to tell him that his grandfather was dead. It was Nanny Lightbody who told him later that Grandpapa had 'gone away' and, as best she could, explained something of what 'going away' meant.

With his grandfather's death and his mother's accession to the throne, Charles was now next in the line of succession. A Prince from birth, he was now also Duke of Cornwall, the twenty-fourth holder of that ancient title, and the very youthful owner of the estate which had been originally created by Edward III so that his son could live in a style befitting the Black Prince.

The Duchy of Cornwall extends to some 130,000 acres spread throughout half-a-dozen counties, not forgetting the Isles of Scilly. Its revenues come from farms and cottage rents, quarries and oyster beds, to say nothing of first refusal of any whales washed up on the Cornish coast, as well as from the rents of flats and office blocks occupying some forty acres just south of the Thames in London. All of which made the three-year-old inheritor of the title a potentially wealthy man whose riches have been piling up over all the years since.

As part of the deal made between Monarch and Parliament when the Queen first came to the throne in 1952 it was agreed that the bulk of the Duchy's revenues—eight-ninths each year—should go to the state until Charles reached the age of eighteen. Eighteen because that is the time when an heir to Britain's throne comes of age in the sense that a Regent is no longer considered necessary in the event of succeeding to the throne.

The Duchy's revenues, at the time of that original agreement, were around £90,000 a year. So it looked as though the boy Charles would have something like £10,000 a year to stow away in his princely piggy-bank for the future. In fact, he was to get a good deal more than that over the years. Judicious management of the estate, the modernization and conversion of many of its properties, particularly those in London, coupled with the effects of inflation, were to see its revenues shoot up and up, with Charles' one-ninth share increasing in proportion. By his twenty-first birthday, when he came into the entire revenues of the Duchy, these had already risen to £220,000 a year and were still rising. Following the precedent set by an earlier Duke of Cornwall, the great-uncle who ended up as Duke of Windsor, Charles voluntarily surrendered half his Duchy income to the Treasury each year in lieu of income tax. His great-uncle, in fact, had surrendered only one-third. Such was the effect of inflation, however, that Charles could surrender half and still be left with far more than his great-uncle had.

The financial calculations of his Duchy income are complicated. Each year he draws some money on account plus any amount brought forward when the figures for the previous year are finally worked out. The effect of this was that he received a total of £306,328 in 1979 and a total of £550,445 in 1980 with something like £370,000 still left to be brought forward to 1981, plus whatever he arranged to draw on account that year.

Tax-wise, he gets off fairly lightly. Anyone else in Britain with an unearned income of half a million pounds would be left with little more than quarter of that after paying income tax and investment income surcharge. Charles has half. Conversely, to be left with £275,000, as Charles was after giving half to the Treasury in 1980, anyone else would have to start not with £550,000 but something in excess of a million pounds.*

As we have already shown, Charles had known from the tender age of two that he was someone rather special; not merely Charles but 'Prince Charles'. A piping 'That's me, Mummy' in church one Sunday when prayers were being said

*CALCULATIONS BASED ON UNITED KINGDOM TAX RATES FOR 1980-1.

for, among others, His Royal Highness the Duke of Cornwall also reveals at least a childish understanding of the enhanced status which was his on his grandfather's death.

It was around this time that he also realized that his mother was the Queen. This important piece of information was passed on to him not by his parents, but a friendly palace footman when Charles came across him brushing one of the royal robes.

'What are you doing?' Charles wanted to know.

The footman explained that he was getting the robe ready for the Queen to wear at her coronation.

'Who is the Queen?' Charles asked, puzzled.

The footman told him.

If Charles can remember the view from his pram in babyhood, he can probably also remember something of what he saw as he stood on a footstool sandwiched between Granny (the Queen Mother) and Aunt Margo at his mother's coronation ceremony in Westminster Abbey. And it was perhaps Granny who first explained to him, in the course of the ceremony, that he would be the next King, though at four he can have had little real understanding of what a King —or Queen—was. That understanding was to come slowly and gradually over the years ahead. There was, as Charles himself has also said, no single moment in time when he was given a blinding insight into the meaning of monarchy and let out an ecstatic yell of 'Yippee!'

'Slowly you get an idea that you have a certain duty and responsibility.'

The full understanding of who he was and what lay ahead came to him in a succession of jigsaw-like bits and pieces... sentries presenting arms and policemen saluting when a small boy passes by; being told to take a sweet from your mouth before the car glides to a halt and people get a close look at you; having to wait while Mummy is formally piped aboard the royal yacht and has been greeted by the ship's officers before you can be reunited with her after six months of separation; being allowed to take a sneak peep at such great men as Winston Churchill when they visit the palace on official occasions. Childlike, you may be more interested in some of the funny hats worn by the ladies on such occasions, but something else—some intangible sense of royal purpose—is absorbed also.

Whatever other 'mistakes' the royal parents may feel they made in the upbringing of Prince Charles, it cannot be said that they hustled him into public life at too young an age. On the contrary, they were concerned to see that he was kept out of it. Early attempts to enrol him in juvenile or charitable organizations were politely, but firmly, discouraged. 'There'll be plenty of time for that later on', Philip chided a man who wondered why Charles and Anne, as children, were not at a royal garden party.

Even his creation of Prince of Wales did not involve him personally, which was perhaps just as well, he was embarrassed enough merely watching the ceremony on television.

Edward I, if historic legend can be believed, created the first-ever Prince of Wales by standing on the battlements of Caernarvon Castle with his infant son in his arms and uttering the stirring cry, 'I give you a Prince of Wales born in your own country.' But Edward did not have all the gimmickry of present-day communications at his command. Elizabeth II does, though the original idea is more likely to have been her husband's than her own. It takes an agile brain like Philip's to conceive a way whereby the monarch can make her son Prince of Wales without the necessity for either of them being present. So on the final day of the Commonwealth Games in Cardiff we find Philip standing in for his schoolboy son and a tape recorder in place of the Queen, who was at home in Buckingham Palace, convalescing from an operation designed to relieve her sinusitis. All of which did not prevent the predominantly Welsh crowd, fervently royalist in those less nationalistic days, from displaying their emotional loyalty with a throaty chorus of *God Bless The Prince Of Wales* as the disembodied, tape-recorded voice of Her Majesty proclaimed the fact that she was elevating young Charles to the dignity of Prince of Wales that day.

The enthusiasm, because the crowd was smaller, was on a lesser scale on the headmaster's study at Cheam into which Charles and a handful of classmates had been herded to watch the occasion on television. Even so, Charles wriggled uneasily on his chair and blushed to the roots of his overlong hair as the headmaster and the rest hip-hip-hoorayed him.

'When he is grown up,' said his mother's tape-recorded voice, 'I will present him to you at Caernarvon.'

His elevation to Prince of Wales brought further requests for the boy to go here and there, do this or that. His parents would not have it. Even a suggestion that, as Duke of Cornwall rather than Prince of Wales, he should open a new bridge in Cornwall brought only a parental headshake. Nor would they agree that he should start going on their overseas tours with them. After all, as a royal aide pointed out, he was not part of the royal dinner service to be carted around wherever his mother went. It is seldom that the Queen herself has spoken out publicly on such personal family matters, but she did in her fireside chat that Christmas. 'We believe that public life is not a fair burden to place on growing children.'

But just as the son of a farmer will begin to learn about crops and cattle because of the environment around him, so Charles began to learn about royal duty and responsibility, to absorb a sense of dynasty and destiny. The 'fellow with three heads' in the Grand Corridor of Windsor Castle, he found out, was his ancestor, Charles I, a triple portrait painted by Van Dyck. There was a visit to St George's Chapel where he was shown one of the knightly stalls and told, 'That will be yours one day.' He was told what was involved in being a Knight of the Garter and something of the other Orders of Chivalry. During school vacations there were visits to such places as the Houses of Parliament and Westminster Abbey. Reading the lesson during a carol service at Sandringham one Christmas was by way of being an introduction to all the speech-making that would come later. He was already accustomed to the cheers of the crowd and had learned to acknowledge them with a royal wave copied from his father. When his schoolmates pulled his leg about this, he defended himself with a muttered, 'It's only polite.'

Pampered though he was in some directions in childhood, those hallmarks of royalty—politeness and punctuality—had been drilled into him early on. Even as quite a small boy, he would charge along the station platform, dragging an even smaller Anne along with him, to say thank you to the engine driver at the end of a train journey.

It was perhaps less with the intention of training him to follow in her footsteps than of giving him a special treat after he had had his appendix whipped out that the Queen arranged for him to be present at one of those palace luncheons which supposedly help to keep the Royals in touch with public thinking. He was thirteen at the time and did his schoolboy best to uphold the royal end of the lunchtime conversation with such intellectual heavyweights as the chairman of the BBC, the editor of the *Church Times,* the boss of Vickers and a former chairman of the Trades Union Congress.

But his parents would still permit no interruption with his schooling. Charles, during his early years at Gordonstoun, might have preferred it if they had. It was not until he was sixteen that royal chores were allowed to intrude into his school-boy life and that the training for his future public role took a more specific turn. Looking more than ever like a junior edition of his dead grandfather, King George VI, he joined the rest of his family in their state funeral tribute to Sir Winston Churchill. For the first time he attended a meeting of the council which oversees the running of his Duchy of Cornwall estate, listening carefully as his father and the others discussed such varied topics as the fishing rights of the Helford River, what to do with a farm in Devon and a house in the Scilly Isles, and how about pulling down some of those Victorian properties in Kennington and replacing them with a modern office block. During the brief period of his mother's annual stay in Edinburgh's gloomy Palace of Holyroodhouse he was given a day off from school to attend a

Left: The music-loving Prince

Below: Following in his father's footsteps, Prince Charles enjoys a game of polo

Left: A good listener and a good speaker, listening to Harry Secombe at a reception of the London Welsh Association

Below: Addressing the Institute of Directors in the Albert Hall

Prince Charles being awarded his pilot's wings at a passing-out parade at Cranwell, after completing a five-month flying course, August 1971

A helicopter pilot in another Service

Left: The Prince with an American girl, Laura Jo Watkins, in an officers' club at San Diego

Below: The Prince dancing during the Fiji Islands centenary of association with Britain in 1974

Prince Charles takes a tough commando assault course in his stride as he tackles a tree-to-tree rope walk at the Royal Marine training centre at Lympstone, Devon. He described the assault course as "a most horrifying expedition".

The Queen Mother shortly before her seventy-fifth birthday
with her eldest grandchild

Prince Charles salutes as he boards the minehunter HMS *Bronington* in early 1976 to take command

royal garden party with a specially youthful guest list. He stood in line with his parents to welcome the guests, but one young lady, after shaking hands with the Queen and Prince Philip, somehow overlooked the teenage Charles. 'Wait a minute. What about me?' he called after her.

Automatically on his eighteenth birthday he became one of the Counsellors of State who act for the Queen if she is ill or out of the country, displacing the then Prince Richard of Gloucester, and the following year, when his mother went to Canada, he served in this capacity along with his grandmother, his aunt (Princess Margaret) and his great-uncle (the then Duke of Gloucester).

Between Gordonstoun and Cambridge part of his vacation was also taken up with royal duty, his father whizzing him around Britain on a sort of crash course designed to familiarize him with various aspects of everyday life. From London to Wales they dashed over a period of some eleven days, from the Midlands to Scotland, calling in at government departments and newspaper offices, going down a coalmine in Nottingham, exploring a new subway in London and British Rail's continental depot.

Conditioned by upbringing and environment, it apparently did not seem at all odd to Charles that on one day, wearing a safety helmet and protective overalls, he should watch miners rip coal from the earth, and that on another he should have a blue and gold embroidered garter buckled round one leg as part of a quaint medieval ceremony dating back some six centuries. The garter-buckling ceremony took place at Windsor when his mother made him a Knight Companion of the Order of the Garter, that small and select company set up by Edward III to safeguard the honour of either his wife, Queen Philippa, or his favourite, the Countess of Salisbury—history is not at all clear as to exactly whose honour was involved—after the lady concerned somehow lost her own garter during a courtly romp.

Another switch: another contrast. From medieval memory to modern make-believe; from Edward III and his lady's garter to evening dress and the

Royal Film Performance. The film selected that year for the modern equivalent of the medieval command performance was, appropriately enough, that love-story of medieval Italy, *Romeo and Juliet*. Often it is father Philip who holds things up on official occasions and keeps his wife waiting. This time it was son Charles, chatting busily away with actress Joan Collins while mum tapped a toe in mild impatience. Father walks back and suggests, gently, that they hurry it up. Charles blushes—perhaps at the idea of being treated like a child while talking to someone as delectable as Miss Collins. But he refuses to be hurried and mum and dad continue to wait while he finishes his conversation.

More and more he found himself either deputizing for his mother or accompanying her on official occasions selected to broaden and complete his monarchial education. He flew out to Australia to represent her at the funeral of Harold Holt, the Australian prime minister. He was on hand to help her greet Richard Nixon when the American president visited Britain. He took part in the traditional carriage drive at Royal Ascot and rode with his mother to the State Opening of Parliament. He accompanied her on an official visit to the Isles of Scilly (which form part of his Duchy of Cornwall) where he met one of your not-so-average holiday families, the Wilsons, father Harold,* mother Mary, son Giles and labrador Paddy.

A banner with a strange device—*Ie Liek Mie Kween*—greeted the royal party as they went ashore from *Britannia*.

'Is that the Cornish language?' Charles inquired, though, as Duke of Cornwall, he really ought to have known better.

He was told that it was something called 'the initial teaching alphabet'.

He was to receive a much less civil and more embarrassing reply when he posed a somewhat similar question in Cardiff ahead of his investiture as Prince of Wales.** He was outside the Welsh Office at the time and greeted by another banner he did not understand. Also by a

*THEN PRIME MINISTER
**APPENDIX III

degree of cat-calling and boo-ing from a bunch of demonstrators who clearly did not want an Englishman as Prince of Wales.

As he has shown time and again, Charles does not lack guts. He nerved himself to walk over to the demonstrators and take things up with them.

'What does it say?' he asked, pointing to the banner.

'You're supposed to be the Prince of Wales. You should speak Welsh,' retorted one of the demonstrators, ignoring the fact that some seventy-five per cent of present-day Welsh do not speak their native tongue either. 'It refers to Llewelyn, Prince of Wales, massacred by the English.' He made it sound as though it had just happened instead of taking place seven centuries ago.

'I am learning Welsh,' Charles informed him, 'but I am not very well up in Welsh history.'

'I can believe that,' the demonstrator shot back at him. 'You got into university with two poor examination results.'

A case-hardened politician would have

grinned it off. Philip would probably have given the demonstrators the benefit of his sometimes acid tongue. Charles, today, would doubtless handle the same sort of situation with charm and humour. But at that time he could only blush, look uncomfortable and walk away.

'I admire your guts, but not your job', another of the demonstrators called after him as he moved off.

Discussing the whole incident later, Charles was to shrug it off, commenting that he didn't really feel he could blame people for demonstrating against him. 'They've never seen me before and don't know what I'm like. I've hardly been to Wales and you can't really expect people to be over-zealous about having a so-called English prince.'

As the number of his public engagements steadily increased—dinner with the Honourable Company of Gentlemen-at-Arms, a visit to the Television Centre, attendance at the annual Festival of Remembrance—inevitably his studies were more and more interrupted. For the most part, Charles accepted such interruptions philosophically as simply part of the role to which he had been born and made up the time needed for his degree course where and when he could. But the idea of uprooting himself completely from Trinity just as he had really settled down there and transferring to the University College of Aberystwyth simply so that he could be presented to the Welsh people on investiture day, in paraphrase of Edward I, as 'a Prince of Wales educated (briefly) in your own country and with a smattering of the Welsh tongue' was something else. While he may have appreciated the reasons which required this move, he nevertheless found the whole idea extremely unsettling.

So unsettling indeed, if one of his Trinity contemporaries can be believed, that he was heard to grumble around this time that he was 'tired of the whole business' and wished there was 'an honourable way' to get out of it. Even a prince is human and he may have said something of the sort. If so, it was doubtless—like his loss of temper with the polo commentator years later—no more than a passing squall brought on by the many

201

pressures to which he was subject at the time.

The overture outside the Welsh Office in Cardiff was hardly a good omen for the full investiture production still to come. 'It would be unnatural if one didn't feel apprehension,' Charles was to confess. 'One always wonders what is going to happen at this sort of thing. As long as I don't get too much covered in egg and tomato...'

It seemed at one time as if there might be worse dangers ahead than merely egg and tomato. In the run-up to the investiture there were also a few bombs tossed about by a handful of young Welsh hotheads who seemed to think a human life or two, including their own, of less value than the privilege of being able to speak their own musical but (to the outsider) totally incomprehensible language and the indignity of having a London-born prince thrust upon them.

If he was personally sorry to be switching from Trinity College, Cambridge, to the University College of Aberystwyth for a seven-week course in the Welsh language and Welsh history, friends at

Trinity were no less sorry to see him go. They gave him what they styled an 'exiled to Aberystwyth' dinner to speed him on his way. His arrival at Aberystwyth was rather less cordial. While he was greeted by cheers and cries of 'Welcome, little love' (that being the nearest translation from the Welsh) by the crowd of some 500 people who gathered to witness his arrival, there was also noticeable disapproval in some quarters. A Welsh-language bookshop displayed for sale grinning caricatures of someone called 'Carlo' and a satirical song with the same title was soon to become top of the local pops.

Translated into English, part of the song went something like this:

I have a friend who lives in Buckingham Palace
And Carlo Windsor is his name.
The last time I went round to his house,
His mother answered the door and said:
'Carlo, Carlo, Carlo is playing polo today;
Carlo is playing polo with his daddy.'
So come all ye serfs of Wales and join

203

in the chorus,
At last you have a prince in this land of song.

Probably it sounded better in the original Welsh.

Four students with strong Welsh Nationalist sympathies barricaded themselves in a lecture room at University College and announced that they were on hunger strike in protest at his coming. A Continental magazine, eager to cash in on all this opposition, offered a handsome reward to anyone who could come up with a photograph of Charles being smacked in the face by a Welsh Nationalist. Alternatively, they were prepared to settle for a photograph of him being kissed by a pretty girl.

There were other hazards apart from being smacked in the face or being kissed by a pretty girl. To safeguard Charles against any possibility, some seventy plain-clothes detectives took up duty in Aberystwyth with a bomb-disposal squad on standby.

Why the whole investiture idea was not quietly abandoned in the face of such threats of violence is a little puzzling. Creating Charles Prince of Wales, which had been done years before while he was still a schoolboy at Cheam, was surely enough to satisfy age-old tradition. There was little enough that was traditional about the idea that he must be ceremoniously invested at Caernarvon into the bargain. Any tradition attached to that would seem to have gone back only just over half a century to when a youthful and highly embarrassed Duke of Windsor was decked out in satin knee-breeches and an ermine-trimmed cloak simply, it seems, to help the political ambitions of the wily Lloyd George. Certainly the Royals themselves do not appear to have been over-enthused. Charles muttered that he would be 'glad when it was all over,' his father queried whether the whole business wasn't just a little bit archaic and his mother, showing herself to be more in touch with public opinion than some people might think, wondered if it was not the wrong time to be seen throwing so much money around on another spot of royal pageantry.

However, a public opinion poll taken

at that time came up with some interesting statistics. Over three-quarters of the Welsh people—76 per cent in fact—declared themselves, on the basis of that poll, to be in favour of an investiture. Curiously enough, enthusiasm was lower in both England (67 per cent for) and Scotland (65 per cent).

If the Queen queried whether too much money was being spent, the late Duke of Norfolk, who masterminded the whole business, took the opposite view, grumbling that the £200,000 allotted was barely sufficient to put on a proper show. Another £50-100,000, he said, would have enabled him to introduce 'a spot more glamour'—a remark which was calculated to make the ceremony of investiture sound rather like a new production of the Folies Bergère—and he would have been far happier with a cool half a million at his disposal.

With Norfolk as master of ceremonies and the Queen's brother-in-law, the Earl of Snowdon, as its main designer, the ceremony of investiture became, if not a Welsh version of the Folies Bergère, certainly a quaint mixture of ancient and modern, a cross between medieval pageantry and a present-day television spectacular, the Tudor outfits of the Yeoman of the Guard, the Household Cavalry in their glinting breastplates and nodding plumes, the State Trumpeters silhouetted against the ramparts and the Welsh Druids in their white robes contrasting oddly with the battery of television cameras, the pop-art design of the Prince of Wales' feathers and the pexiglassed royal rostrum erected in the upper ward of Edward I's crumbling castle at Caernarvon.

If our writing has somehow mixed the lyrical with the comical, then so did parts of the ceremony. Lord Snowdon, in his role as Constable of the castle, contrived to look like a cross between a medieval courtier and an hotel commissionaire in a self-designed outfit in hunting green with a zip-fronted tunic and tasselled belt. The Royals themselves settled for something simpler. Philip wore the uniform of a Field Marshal while the Queen opted for a knee-length Hartnell-designed coat and dress in pale yellow. Charles was saved from the embarrassment of donning satin knee-breeches by his appointment, shortly before the ceremony, as Colonel-in-Chief of the Royal Regiment of Wales. Just as he had followed his father to Cheam and Gordonstoun, so he now followed him to his tailors, emerging on the big day in regimental No 1 blues.

The violence of the anti-investiture brigade continued right up to the day of the ceremony. In the three weeks immediately preceding the ceremony there were four bomb incidents in Cardiff alone, bomb No 4 blowing a hole in the wall of the post office. 'Someone is going to get killed if this doesn't stop,' said the city's chief constable. It didn't stop and someone was killed. In the Denbighshire town of Abergele in the early hours of investiture day, two would-be bombers blew themselves up with their own bomb.

The train conveying the royal party to Caernarvon was halted for fifty minutes at Crewe while explosive experts dealt with a limpet 'bomb' attached to the bridge which carried the railway line over the River Dee at Chester. However, the four sticks of 'gelignite' turned out to be nothing more lethal than ordinary household candles. As Charles drove to the castle there was an explosion in some railway sidings nearby. By the time the Queen and Prince Philip followed him bombs had given way to a solitary egg. And even that failed to reach its target. Police dived into the crowd, though more to protect the egg-thrower from those around him than to safeguard the Royals.

The population of Caernarvon that day was swollen from its normal 9,060 to an estimated 50,000. Local traders were disappointed that the crowds were not larger and blamed it on the telly. The six-hour investiture transmission kept some 19 million people glued to their sets elsewhere in Britain. Nevertheless, some local traders and most landladies did very well indeed. Guest houses bulged at the seams, some at prices more than double the usual rate. Souvenirs of the occasion—mugs and goblets, plates and vases, pencils and key-rings, ash-trays and calendars, tea towels and miniature plots of land with decorated scroll deeds (at ten dollars a time for the benefit of visiting Americans)—sold like the proverbial hot cakes.

The total of uniformed policemen and plainclothes detectives drafted in almost outnumbered the native population. And the cost of security precautions must have sent total expenditure soaring well beyond the intended £200,000. A defence boom was strung across the water approach to the castle, helicopters fluttered around overhead, minesweepers patrolled out at sea and frogmen inspected the hull of the royal yacht, berthed off Holyhead, against the possibility of limpet mines. Civil aircraft were banned in the vicinity of the castle and rooftops were checked for snipers. Military bandsmen arriving for the ceremony had to open their instrument cases before they were allowed in, picnic hampers were searched and women had to reveal the contents of their handbags. Even Princess Margaret was stopped by a conscientious security guard and asked to show her pass.

Only 4000 tickets had been handed out for the actual ceremony as against the 11,000 issued in 1911. Those allowed inside, including Charles' old nanny, were privileged to witness a ceremony which, due to the obvious sincerity of its two principal participants, Prince Charles and the Queen, managed somehow to rise above its three-ring-circus packaging. For Charles, there was a long, nervous wait in the dank dungeon of the Chamberlain Tower before receiving his cue to take the centre of the stage.

Blushing at being the centre of so much attention, he walks slowly to the rostrum. A long wait while the Letters Patent are read in both languages, English and Welsh. Charles looks round idly and catches his father's eye. Philip grins encouragingly and Charles grins back. But a grin is out of place on this most solemn occasion. Hurriedly he wipes the slate of his face clean.

Charles kneels before his mother, places his hands between hers and utters the somewhat ambiguous words of the vow of allegiance:

'I, Charles, Prince of Wales, do become your liege man of life and limb and earthly worship, and faith and truth will I bear unto you, to live and die against all manner of folks.'

The Queen buckles on his sword and places his made-to-measure coronet on his head. A gadget known as a *conformateur,* and looking rather like some tool of torture from a medieval dungeon, had been borrowed from Lock the 'By Appointment' hatters to measure his head and he had worn the resulting coronet, with its £3000-worth of diamonds and emeralds, around his palace home in advance of the ceremony to get used to the feel of the thing. The Queen next drapes him with a purple and ermine mantle, pops on his ring and hands him his sceptre.

Inevitably, something went wrong. Charles sat on his speech and had to wriggle it from under his posterior as unobtrusively as possible. It must be unique for a professional entertainer to rate a mention in the midst of so much pomp and circumstance. But that latter-day royal jester, Harry Secombe, received one by implication even if he was not actually named. In a speech which extended and developed the 'sea of song' phrase which a previous Prince of Wales had learned from Lloyd George over half-a-century earlier, Charles eulogized the Welsh heritage:

'A heritage which dates back into the mists of ancient British history, that has produced many brave men, princes, poets, bards, scholars and, more recently, great singers, a very memorable Goon and eminent film stars.'

Secombe himself, bogged down in heavy traffic on his way to Caernarvon, heard the speech over his car radio.

And so, finally, to the banner-hung balcony of St Eleanor's Gate where the Queen, after the manner of Edward I all those centuries before, presents the freshly invested Prince of Wales to his Welsh subjects as 'my most dear son'.

During the four days immediately following the ceremony Charles toured his principality.

'Despite the strictest security precautions, bombs are exploding and houses and cars burning along the Prince's entire route. Police have been rushed off their feet de-fusing mines.'

The words are not ours, but those of

Radio Moscow.

The reality was rather different. True, an army van did burst into flames and a soldier inside it was burned to death, but it appears that the man was drunk and accidentally contrived his own tragic end. A suspicious-looking biscuit tin was blown up by a bomb disposal team just before Charles crossed the stone bridge over the River Conway near Betws-y-Coed and elsewhere equally suspicious-looking wires connected to a telegraph pole were quickly snipped. But both incidents appear to have been no more than hoaxes, as the 'bomb' found in a railway subway at Port Talbot most certainly was.

Far from being the near-civil war situation invented by Radio Moscow, the tour turned out an overwhelming success. So many people wanted to pump his hand that Charles, not yet hardened to multiple handshaking as his mum and dad are, had to have heat treatment to an inflamed shoulder.

At one stage he found himself besieged by so many well-wishers that he fell behind schedule. Told that he would miss a fly-past being staged by the Fleet Air Arm if he didn't hurry things up, he retorted that it was far more important to 'meet the people'. In Rhyl his attention was caught by a cry of anguish from a small boy who had somehow contrived to trap his foot under one of the crush barriers. Charles turned back and lifted the barrier clear of the boy's foot himself.

The tour ended in Cardiff where, in contrast to the somewhat boorish treatment meted out to him all those months before, he was now accorded the Freedom of the City. There was only one objector, a lone youth bearing a placard inscribed 'Home Rule for Wales'. He was booed and threatened by those around him until the placard was finally snatched from his grasp and torn to shreds by an older man who said: 'I'm his father.'

'You have won the hearts of all of us,' Charles was told by the city's lord mayor, Lincoln Hallinan, following a service at the war memorial and the watching crowd, in the Welsh fashion, underlined the truth of what he said by bursting into a spontaneous rendering of *God Bless The Prince Of Wales.*

7 Sportsman

Like father, like son, Prince Charles, like Prince Philip, apparently sees no contradiction in banging away at pheasants and grouse with a shotgun while at the same time urging upon other people the necessity to conserve wild life, as he does eloquently and emotively in the foreword to a book entitled *The Living World Of Animals*.

'No amount of human ingenuity can resurrect an extinct species,' he writes, 'but it can defend one from extinction if enough forethought and determination are employed in its defence.

'I have always had an interest in wild life—one which I have probably inherited from my father. I can never fail to be fascinated by and grateful for the incredible complexities of nature. A world deprived of any more of those animals would not be a world that I could care to extol.'

However, there is no record that he has ever defended his occasional shooting forays in the same way that Princess Anne and husband Mark have defended their fox-hunting. To Mark, the fox is 'a pest', while Anne thinks that those who criticize fox-hunting should first ask themselves how their breakfast egg and the chicken in their Kentucky Fried Chicken are produced.

If put to it, Charles could perhaps defend the shooting of pheasants, partridges and grouse in much the same way. As species, they are certainly in no great danger of extinction at the present time. On the contrary, in order to have something to shoot at, twentieth century *homo upper-class Britannicus* continues to breed and rear them in greater numbers than Mother Nature could conceivably manage on her own. Moreover, like the chicken in Kentucky Fried Chicken, they are killed for food in the sense that those knocked off at Sandringham and Balmoral are either sold commercially or go into the palace deep-freeze to be served up at future state banquets.

It could hardly be expected that Charles would see things in any other way when he has been brought up from childhood in an atmosphere of what some people know as field sports and others, more dramatically and emotionally, as 'blood sports'.

Rightly or wrongly, field sports are part of his royal heritage. If you go back in history you will find that there were areas of medieval Britain which were specially preserved so that the monarch of the day could hunt stage and the like. More recently, every king since the days of portly Edward VII has blasted away with guns. Indeed, Edward made a considerable production of it, dressing his gamekeepers in suits of green velveteen, his beaters in rural smocks and, in company with his society friends, slaughtering up to 2000 birds a day.* George V and George VI continued to practice, though less spectacularly and without too much criticism. Royalty was not then

*A DESCRIPTION OF A DAY'S SHOOTING WITH EDWARD VII CAN BE FOUND IN OUR BOOK *BERTIE AND ALIX*

the critical target it has tended to become in the last generation.

Prince Philip, by contrast, has been fairly well lambasted over the years for his shooting exploits. His deer-stalking has been termed 'loathsome', Italian newspapers talked of 'butchery' after a day's shooting in that country in company with business tycoon Vittorio Necchi, and the League Against Cruel Sports has waxed eloquent about what it has called his 'trigger-happy exploits'. The odd thing about all this is that Philip would perhaps never have become a shooting man had he not married into the Royal Family. Before that he had done only a little rough shooting, rabbits and suchlike, with a borrowed gun, but nothing more. It was not a way of life which particularly attracted him. But in the new and more rarefied circles in which he found himself moving when he first began courting the then Princess Elizabeth, shooting was the done thing. So Philip took it up.

On his mother's side too, Charles was raised from childhood against a similar background. The Queen, if she has never banged away at grouse and pheasants, was taught how to stalk a stag in her early teens, quickly became a crack shot with a hunting rifle and has since bagged herself a fair quota of venison.

Even before he went to school, during Christmas visits to the royal estate at Sandringham, Charles would be out in the shooting field, helping the beaters to put up the birds, racing around as small boys will with a stick clapped to his shoulder and shouts of 'bang-bang,' joining in the excitement of counting the bag at the end of the day. Listening to his father and others, he soon became as familiar with the jargon of the shooting field as other small boys are with the language of football. Like other small boys too, he enjoyed mimicking his elders, asking the head gamekeeper at Sandringham 'Are there a lot of pheasants this year?' or telling the kennel-man, 'I must come along and look at the dogs.'

His father taught him the correct way to hold a gun, how to cast for trout— a special treat at Balmoral was to have the catch for a barbecue picnic—and took him punt-gunning on the Norfolk Broads where he stayed at a local inn and helped to retrieve the dead birds. He was ten when he shot his first grouse on the heather-clad moors at Balmoral. He ran excitedly indoors, dead bird in hand, and asked the chef if he would cook it for his supper.

News of that particular childhood exploit went unnoticed outside the royal circle, unreported and consequently uncriticized. Not so a subsequent sortie after pheasant at Sandringham with Lord Brabourne's son, Norton Knatch-bull for company, and Prince Philip as tutor. This found its way into the news-papers and resulted in a protest from the League Against Cruel Sports, the first of several over the years. Indeed, the news soon after that Charles had shot his first stag in the hills around Balmoral saw the League delivering a resolution to the boy's mother in which it 'vigorously con-demned' what had taken place. Protests and resolutions concerning the upbring-ing of Charles and Anne were not all that uncommon of course. There was even one from the Lord's Day Observance

Society protesting about the 'desecration of the Sabbath' when word leaked out that Aunt Margo had bought her nephew and niece an ice-cream apiece one Sunday.

The royal parents appear to have taken little or no notice of such protests. Philip continued to teach his son to shoot and fish. The Christmas following his thirteenth birthday Charles was considered old enough and experienced enough to become a member of his father's shooting parties upon occasion. Later still he inherited his dead grandfather's guns and was also outfitted with his own gundog, a black labrador named Flash. If Charles, at first, would seem to have had some difficulty in handling the dog, his mother did not. A sharp whistle from her was always sufficient to bring it quickly to heel.

As far as Philip was concerned, teaching Charles to shoot was merely another step forward in shaping the boy into the type of son he most wanted. Charles was only three when his father gave him his first swimming lesson in the heated pool at the rear of the palace. Thereafter swimming became a regular part of the daily curriculum. Every day, as soon as he was through with his work, Philip would take the boy along to the pool for another lesson.

Charles had his first mount, a Shetland pony, at around the same age. His mother and a groom shared the initial task of teaching him to ride. And there were always royal aides to take over his tuition on days when his parents were not available, Philip's secretary, Michael Parker, for swimming; the Crown Equerry, Lieutenant-Colonel Sir John Miller for riding; and Rear Admiral Sir Christopher Bonham-Carter for angling.

As a small boy, Charles was inclined to be rather nervous of horses, a fact of which sister Anne, always completely at home on the back of a horse, was not slow to take advantage. One of her favourite tricks, when the pair of them were out riding together, was to drop back slightly, then lean over and give her brother's mount a thwack on the rump, causing it to break into an unexpected canter which had young Charles clinging on for dear life.

Philip believes in youngsters learning early. Later, he has said, there is more of a sense of embarrassment over mistakes and learning becomes that much more difficult. So even before Charles went to Cheam his father was taking him sailing more or less regularly, in a racing catamaran on Loch Muick when the family were on holiday at Balmoral and aboard the Dragon-class *Bluebottle* at Cowes. Whatever he has become since, Charles initially was not a very good sailor and the enjoyment he derived from sailing with dad was sometimes offset by a tendency to seasickness when the weather was rough and the sea choppy.

Charles, by the time he went to Cheam, could already swim like a fish and at Gordonstoun, later, he was to gain a bronze medal for life-saving. In other respects, he was hardly the athletic Prince Philip all over again. Philip, as a schoolboy, excelled at athletics, cricket and hockey. Charles never played hockey in schooldays—though he has played some aggressive games of deck hockey since in the Navy—and it cannot honestly be said that he really enjoyed any other of the normal schoolboy team games. He played both cricket and soccer at Cheam but hardly covered himself with glory at either. His final year there found him captain of the school's football team. It is perhaps a period of his young life he would prefer to forget. Under his captaincy—he played at centre half—the Cheam eleven not only lost every game, but, judging by the scores, by fairly decisive margins. Goals for—4; goals against—82. However, the school magazine was perhaps unfair in querying what the youthful skipper had been up to, to permit such a disaster to take place. There were, after all, ten other players in the side, including the goalkeeper who let through those 82 shots.

At Gordonstoun, even more than at Cheam, Charles felt himself to be living in the shadow of his athletic father, who was captain of both cricket and hockey in his day. Cast in a different, less athletic mould, Charles had little hope of emulating him—and none at all of outshining him—and it speaks volumes for his strength of character that he did at least try. Rugby, like soccer and cricket, was not a game which particularly enthused him, yet he played it regularly, perhaps in part because he felt that something of the sort was expected of him as his father's son. The attitude of some of those he played against often turned the game into something approaching an ordeal for him. To them it was almost a point of schoolboy honour to tackle their future King as robustly as possible at every opportunity, the more so if the pitch was 'sticky' and there was a chance of rubbing the royal nose well and truly in the mud. In the words of one of his team-mates, Charles was usually 'the most marked player on the field', not because he was especially dangerous in his role of lock forward but because he was who he was. He was equally the muddiest and most bruised player to limp off the pitch at the end of the game and there was one occasion, during the playing season of 1966, when he ended up with a broken nose.

He played cricket at Gordonstoun too, as he had done at Cheam and with hardly more success. Despite private coaching, he was not really the stuff of which youthful cricketers are made. In time he realized this himself and eventually abandoned cricket in favour of tennis, a game he also played occasionally during his undergraduate days at Trinity. Appearances on the cricket field since Gordonstoun have been rare indeed, though he was persuaded into taking part in a country house match while staying with his relatives, the Brabournes, in 1968. Taking the field in borrowed flannels and boots against a team of Grand Prix drivers, he managed to score a total of twenty, including an unexpectedly well-hit six, before being caught by Bruce McLaren from the bowling of the late Graham Hill.

But if Charles, during his schooldays, did not exactly shine at cricket, soccer or rugby, there were other directions in which he fared better. He became a reasonably proficient skier despite the harassment from photographers and sightseers which marred his first lessons and, for his age, an excellent shot. He had his first driving lessons when he was still too short for his feet to reach the pedals, sitting between his father's long legs in a Land Rover and learning to steer while Philip did the necessary footwork. Before he was even in his teens, let alone of an age to be let loose in a motor vehicle on the public highway, he was sufficiently adept to drive his parents along the six miles of private road which link Balmoral Castle with the Queen Mother's house at Birkhall.

Similarly he had his first polo lessons while still a schoolboy at Cheam, though not yet on horseback. His father had a miniature mallet fashioned for him and, on weekends when the schoolboy prince was allowed home to Windsor, the pair of them, father and son, would circle each other on bicycles, taking swings at the ball. Practice on a mechanical polo pony which Philip had rigged up in the palace mews to help improve his own game, an ingenious contraption which automatically returned the ball to the player, also benefited Charles.

By the age of thirteen he had graduated to one of his father's polo ponies and, while the eyes of sightseers were focused on a game in which Philip was playing, Charles could slip away to a quiet corner of Smith's Lawn at Windsor for a spot of practice. Beginners at golf, knowing how difficult it is to hit even a stationary ball while standing still, will readily appreciate the problem Charles had at first in hitting a moving ball from the back of a cantering mount. 'It takes time to get the knack', Philip told him encouragingly. However, he had less difficulty, that same day, in taking the wheel of his mother's car and driving it round the ground before reversing neatly into place alongside his father's vehicle.

At eighteen, just ahead of going to Cambridge, he made his début in competition polo, playing beside his father for the Windsor Park team in a Combermere Cup game against Bucket Hill. In the third chukka came the chance he had been waiting for and he scored his first goal. It was initially given as no-goal, but then the judge changed his mind and signalled it good. There were cheers from the crowd and a bellow of 'Well done, Charles. Magnificent stuff' from Colonel Gerard Legh who had himself already scored three goals for Windsor with another to follow. Philip also scored a goal, giving Windsor Park victory by 6 goals to 1½ (Bucket Hill receiving a half-goal handicap).

At Cambridge, where he also played the occasional game of tennis and took up squash, Charles continued his polo playing and gained his university colours, what is known as a 'half Blue'. He played for Cambridge in the 1969 inter-varsity game against Oxford. Cambridge lost by 4-1, but Charles had the satisfaction of scoring his side's only goal.

There were also weekends at Cambridge when, feeling the need to get away from it all, he would take off on his own, with only his detective or a solitary friend for company, and drive north to Sandringham, staying not in the 'Big House' but in an old farmhouse, small by royal standards, which his mother had had renovated for his use on the edge of Wolferton marshes. Here, gun in hand and dog at heel, he would wander for hours through the fields and woods, taking the occasional pot-shot. Similarly at Balmoral, on vacation, he would take off sometimes with only his detective in tow, to stay the night at a quiet inn and spend a few away-from-it-all hours fishing some quiet stream.

He has continued to fish and play polo in the years since leaving Cambridge. There has been a deal of skiing and some sub-aqua diving. In the summer of 1975 he visited the site of the *Mary Rose,* the 91-gun ship which was the pride of Henry VIII's fleet until sunk off Spithead by the French in 1545. Diving with Alexander McKee, the archaeologist who launched the project to raise the vessel— a project, incidentally, to which Prince Philip contributed—Charles went down through some fifty feet of water to take a look at the exposed port side of the vessel and watch a gunport cover being excavated with the aid of an underwater vacuum cleaner. 'Fascinating', he said of the experience.

At heart, he is perhaps what his late grandfather always most wanted to be, a country sportsman. At the time of his betrothal he cited 'love of the outdoors' as the thing he and his bride-to-be had most in common. There is one aspect of his country life, however, which arouses criticism—fox-hunting.

In 1975 he rode out twice with the hounds. The second of these occasions, when he joined Anne and Mark in a ride with the Duke of Beaufort's hounds, caused the RSPCA, which had previously soft-pedalled on the question of royal fox-hunting, suddenly to abandon its earlier almost neutral line and express 'profound regret' at the fox-hunting forays of the royal brother and sister.

Despite this criticism and a subsequent attack by Lord Soper—'Fox-hunting is squalid behaviour which breeds an addiction to violence'—Charles has ridden to hounds occasionally since. But fox-hunting is only one of many princely pursuits—polo, skiing, fishing, pheasant and grouse shooting, windsurfing, cross-country racing and steeplechasing, the last of these a sport prohibited to the late Duke of Windsor when he was Prince of Wales. Indeed, Charles seems willing to chance his arm at anything and everything—tobogganing in Switzerland, camel riding at the International Horse Show, trotting (a sport popular in Australia and America) during a visit to a friend's estate in Scotland where a demonstration was staged. So much so that one newspaper has christened him Action Man, a nickname for which he does not particularly care. Neither, incidentally, does he much like being called Prince, the title by which he is usually addressed in the United States. 'It makes me sound like a police dog,' he says.

Horse racing is his most recent enthusiasm. Taking part in the Madhatters Private Sweepstakes at Plumpton, he finished second to amateur jockey and BBC commentator Derek Thompson. His steeplechasing debut, at Sandown a few days later, was less successful. He came last in a field of four.

Undeterred, he bought a horse of his own, Allibar, for future racing. Sadly, it proved an unfortunate £15,000 investment. Allibar showed promise when Charles rode him into second place in the three-mile Clun Steeplechase at Ludlow, but died dramatically and tragically only four months later as horse and rider were returning from a training canter. Diana, their engagement still a secret, had gone with him to the training stables and watched, apprehensively, as Charles slid from the saddle when Allibar collapsed and died from a heart attack.

Determined to ride in the three-mile Grand Military Cup at Sandown only two weeks later, Charles promptly bought a replacement for Allibar, a 12-year-old named Good Prospect. But two weeks proved hardly sufficient time for horse and rider to become acquainted and at Sandown, with his fiancée, grandmother and Aunt Margo all looking on, he was unseated at the eighteenth fence, bloodying his nose as he hit the ground. 'The only way to learn is to go out and do these things,' he commented, philosophically.

Within days he was not only back in the saddle, but back on the racecourse. 'Have you got the Superglue?' a wag in the crowd called out as he mounted Good Prospect for the Kim Muir Memorial Challenge Cup race at Cheltenham. But even Superglue would have had its work cut out as Good Prospect hit the tenth fence and horse and rider parted company for the second time. There was little damage done, fortunately, except perhaps to Charles's pride. He sat for a few moments beating the ground in frustration with his whip before struggling to his feet. 'Oh, well, live and learn,' he sighed later.

8   Flyer*

The affair was code-named Golden Eagle, which sounds exciting and dramatic enough to have originated in the fertile brain of Alistair MacLean. It was also sufficiently important for an Air Officer Commanding to turn out personally in all the glory of his scrambled egg to give a snappy salute to the Royal Air Force's newest recruit. The recruit, of course, was Flight Lieutenant His Royal Highness the Prince of Wales.

Charles was not issued with an official service number when he entered the Royal Air Force in the Spring of 1971. It was hardly necessary. After all, he was going to be in Air Force uniform a matter of only some six months. Nor did he receive any pay during those six months. This at his own request. Again, it was hardly necessary. Despite the fifty per

*APPENDIX V

237

cent being handed over to the Treasury in lieu of income tax, there was still plenty of money coming in from the Duchy of Cornwall. But he was elevated straightway to the rank of flight lieutenant instead of being enrolled at the lower level of pilot officer or flying officer, which is more usual with new recruits. However, the higher rank was not a sop to his princely status, it was stated, but an acknowledgement of his recently acquired Bachelor of Arts degree and the fact that he could already fly.

Charles learned to fly while at Cambridge. He had his first flip at RAF Tangmere during one of his vacations and enjoyed it so much that subsequently, under the tuiton of Squadron Leader Philip Pinney, he took a course of flying lessons at RAF Oakington in time hard-won from from his degree course at Trinity. He had had some fourteen hours' instruction when Squadron Leader Pinney decided that he was competent enough to go solo. However, when Charles arrived at Oakington on the day of his solo flight, there was too much cloud about to attempt it. Eager to get it over and done with now that the big moment had actually arrived, he and Pinney took off in search of better weather conditions elsewhere. They found them only a few airborne miles away, at RAF Bassingbourn.

Pinney landed the aircraft, a Chipmunk trainer, taxied it to the end of the runway, climbed out, grinned at his royal pupil and said, affably if unobsequiously, 'You're on your own, mate.'

'I only had time for a few butterflies in the tummy', Charles has recalled. 'The moment I was in the air it was absolutely marvellous.'

He soloed successfully and a year later, after graduating to a twin-engined Beagle Basset and having completed the necessary forty hours' flying time, qualified for the Grade A licence of a private pilot. That was early in 1970. The following year, as Golden Eagle, he entered the Royal Air Force and went to the RAF College Cranwell for a conversion course on jets. Most of his training during the six months he was there was on Provost jets, but there was also additional experience for him at the controls of a Phantom bomber, a Vulcan and on Nimrod anti-submarine patrols.

His RAF training, though much of it quickly became routine, had the stimulation of new experience. Charles tackled it, as he tackles everything, industriously and conscientiously, though, being Charles, he could not always resist injecting a spot of light relief...as when he persuaded one of the porters to relay a message over the loud-speaker system instructing cadets who had been issued with a certain type of footwear to hand them in because they had been found to have been fitted with defective heels. Several cadets fell for the gag and duly trotted along with their shoes before they realized that it was April Fools' Day.

The parachute drop which Charles made over the Channel was not an obligatory part of the Cranwell course, but something he simply decided that he would like to do. 'I'm stupid enough to like trying things', he was to say after-wards. The remark is perhaps no more than a typical princely throw-away line designed to cover deeper feelings and the true reason for attempting a parachute drop is perhaps to be found in another remark, less flippant and more revealing, which he has also made.

'I always feel that it is worth challenging yourself and this is what I do most of the time. Perhaps to too great an extent sometimes. Perhaps I push myself too much. But this is my outlook on life.'

He went on to make the comment that 'living dangerously tends to make you appreciate life much more' which we have quoted elsewhere in this book.

There were certainly a few seconds of 'living dangerously' the day he became airborne in an Andover after a brief period of parachute drill at the Royal Air Force training centre at Abingdon.

'All reasonable precautions were taken for his safety', an official statement was to reassure the world later.

Among the 'reasonable precautions' were two preliminary runs by the aircraft during which two Squadron Leaders, Norman Haggett and Arthur Johnson, jumped first to give an indication of wind direction and parachute drift.

The Andover turned for its third run over the target area. Now it was Charles' turn. The Dorset coast had been left behind. There was only sea below...1200 feet below. As at Bassingbourn, before going solo, Charles felt the flutter of 'butterflies in the tummy'. Then the red light came on and he felt a tap on his shoulder.

'Out you go, sir,' said Flight Sergeant Kidd.

Just as the 'butterflies' at Bassingbourn had vanished once he was airborne, so this fresh fluttering disappeared as he jumped, flipping over on to his back as he had been taught, his parachute opening automatically to stream out behind him.

But all the 'reasonable precautions' in the world could not have foreseen or prevented what happened next. His feet, as he fell, were caught in the rigging lines of the parachute.

'Fun-ny,' he has said he remembers thinking. 'They didn't tell me about *this.*'

But though his feet were momentarily caught in the rigging lines, fortunately

242

they did not become entangled. 'They came out very quickly'. Charles remembers. All the same, it must have been—briefly—an experience to provoke more butterflies...'A hairy experience', as Charles himself has referred to it.

His feet free again, he rid himself of the emergency parachute he was also wearing and, as he hit the water of Studland Bay, released the straps to discard the main chute. Within seconds Royal Marines were hauling him into a rubber dinghy and he was on his way to the tender *Aberdovey* and a warming drink.

His conversion course satisfactorily completed, Charles joined his parents on holiday at Balmoral, interrupting his stay there to fly back to Cranwell for graduation day. Wearing the insignia of the Garter over his RAF uniform, he stood crisply to attention to receive his 'wings' from the Chief of the Air Staff, Air Chief Marshal Sir Denis Spotswood.

Prince Philip, who himself, while a schoolboy at Gordonstoun, once toyed with the idea of joining the Royal Air Force before finally deciding on the Royal

Navy instead, looked on in the uniform of a Marshal of the Royal Air Force. Clearly he was highly delighted at his son's achievement. So much so that even his long-standing feud with the press photographers was temporarily forgotten. 'I'll stand on my head if you like', he joked, grinning quizzically, when asked if he would pose with Charles for a photograph.

Charles' brief spell in the Royal Air Force also had a couple of small by-products by way of something fresh in the royal portrait line. Edward Halliday painted him in his flying overalls and wearing his preliminary flying badge, helmet cradled in his arm, while John Hughes-Hallett showed him in full flying gear with his newly won RAF wings on his shoulder. Both portraits were intended for RAF bases.

The RAF report which accompanied the winning of his 'wings' at Cranwell said that Charles had a natural aptitude for flying and excelled at jet-speed aerobatics. He would, it said, make an excellent fighter pilot.

But disappointing though it may have

been to the Royal Air Force, Charles was not to become a fighter pilot. By the time the Hughes-Hallett portrait was unveiled to public gaze he had already discarded his RAF uniform for that of a sub-lieutenant in the Royal Navy (with naval 'wings' on the sleeves in acknowledgement of his flying qualifications).

9   Sailor*

That Charles, despite the occasional spasm of sea-sickness in rough weather when younger, should enter the Navy was perhaps no more than was to be expected. This time he was following not only in his father's footsteps, but in those of his great-uncle, grandfather, great-grandfather and probably a few more Royals and near-Royals if you go back another generation or two.

On both sides of the family he has inherited a long sea-going tradition. His maternal grandfather and great-grandfather were both Navy men, George VI having seen service at the Battle of Jutland as a 21-year-old acting lieutenant during World War I. On the other side of the family, his father also served in the Navy, distinguishing himself for his handling of the searchlights aboard HMS *Valiant* during the night manoeuvres

*APPENDIX V

246

which resulted in the destruction of the Italian fleet at the Battle of Cape Matapan in World War II. Then there was Philip's uncle, Earl Mountbatten of Burma who spent a lifetime afloat, from midshipman at the age of sixteen to First Sea Lord at fifty-five, and before him, Lord Louis' father, Prince Louis of Battenberg (the first Marquess of Milford Haven), the German-born prince who was Britain's First Sea Lord before he was hounded from office by the perhaps natural antipathy towards anyone even remotely German during those chauvinistic days of World War I.

First step in Charles' naval career was a six-week graduate officers' course at Britannia Royal Naval College, Dartmouth, where his mother first fell in love with his father when Philip was himself a young cadet there back in the late 1930s. As if determined to outshine the Royal Air Force, who had produced an Air Officer Commanding to welcome him to Cranwell, the Navy came up with a full trio of top brass—an admiral (Sir Horace Law, Commander in Chief Naval Home Command), a major-general (Sir Julian

Gascoigne, Deputy Lieutenant of Devon) and a civilian mayor (Mr C.F. Mullet)— to greet him on his arrival at Dartmouth. In a degree of ceremonial every bit as archaic as that which surrounded Queen Victoria's eldest son, Bertie (later King Edward VII), when he joined the army a century or more before, Charles had to consent to being driven on to the parade ground in his Aston Martin though he had in fact arrived at Dartmouth the previous day and could just as easily have walked on to the square from his self-contained 'cabin'.

The pomp and circumstance over, the Navy got down to the serious work of turning him into a naval officer. As an acting sub-lieutenant, on a pay scale of £4.50 a day (out of which he had to hand back £1 a day to cover accommodation and messing), he was pushed through a jam-packed course covering square bashing, seamanship, navigation, marine and electrical engineering, administration, management and all the other duties of a divisional officer—'How to deal with people, how to discipline them and be disciplined by them'—together

248

with brief sea-going experience aboard the college's 360-ton minesweeper *Walkerton*.

This time his father was not there to see him take part in the passing-out parade with which the course ended. But great-uncle Lord Louis was, proudly revealing later that the latest sailor prince had come 'top in navigation and top in seamanship'.

The completion of his course at Dartmouth was followed by a few days' leave, after which Charles flew out to Gibraltar to join the 6000-ton guided missile destroyer *Norfolk*. With any other young sub-lieutenant the fact would have gone unnoticed and unremarked on. But Charles was not any other young sub-lieutenant. He was also the Prince of Wales, the Queen's son and Britain's future King. For him to go to Gibraltar, however briefly, was hardly calculated to please Spain's late dictator, General Franco. Mr Michael Atkinson, First Secretary at the British Embassy in Madrid was promptly summoned to the Spanish Foreign Office and handed a note of diplomatic protest: 'The presence in Gibraltar of such a high-ranking member of the British royal family, in demonstrating once more the persistence of a litigious situation, unnecessarily harms national feeling and arouses Spanish public opinion.'

However, Spanish national feeling was not harmed nor Spanish public feeling aroused for long. The *Norfolk,* with Prince Charles aboard, sailed on exercises the following morning. He served with the *Norfolk* from 5th November 1971 to 14th July 1972, acting as second officer of the watch and taking his turn at the helm, working diligently towards gaining his watch-keeping certificate and certificate of naval competence. Like any other officer aboard any other naval vessel, he was 'Sir' to his subordinates. To his equals and those above him he was supposedly 'Prince Charles' but in fact fellow-officers of equal rank soon dropped into the habit of addressing him less reverently as 'Wales'.

Like any other proud mum, the Queen went along to see over her son's ship when it arrived back at Portsmouth. He welcomed her aboard with a strip of sticking plaster adorning his chin, souvenir of a flying ball in a game of polo, and showed her over the ship before having tea with her in the wardroom.

Charles was accommodated at the naval shore establishment known as HMS *Dryad* over the next few months while taking a number of courses in the area, communications, navigation, bridgework and gunnery. Much of it was mathematical, which still did not come easy to him.

He was on his way to gunnery practice during the morning rush hour on one occasion when a car ahead of him braked suddenly and there was a five-car pile-up. However, no one was hurt and damage to vehicles was relatively slight. The drivers of the other cars hopped around making the legal exchanges of names and addresses required in such circumstances. There was no need for Charles to give his name—his face was familiar enough—but the driver who had slammed into him from behind did want to know the name of his insurance company.

'Buckingham Palace,' Charles told him in reply. 'That's the address.'

Another part of his training took place at HMS *Dolphin,* the Gosport shore base, where he was air-locked into the bottom of a 100-ft water tower for submarine escape drill, this in advance of a day to be spent off the Scottish coast in the nuclear submarine *Churchill,* familiarizing himself with the vessel's diving and periscope controls. There was also some familiarization flying with the Royal Navy and the Queen's Flight, and an interim appointment to the coastal mine-sweeper *Glasserton* before joining the frigate *Minerva.*

The next eighteen months, first aboard *Minerva* and then with another frigate of the same class, HMS *Jupiter,* must surely rank in his memory with the months spent at Timbertop in terms of personal happiness. For perhaps the first time since Timbertop he was free to be himself, to act completely naturally without thought of possible consequences. At sea, he was no longer dogged by reporters and photographers, no longer stared at and pointed out by sightseers, no longer concerned that some small action on his part might find its way into the headlines (though inevitably some did in due course) or end up as an unexpected front-page photograph.

With *Minerva* he visited the Caribbean and South America, the United States and Canada. The necessity for performing royal chores here and there in addition to his shipboard duties made for long hours and hard work. But he was never one to shirk either. Calling at the Bahamas, he represented his mother at the independence celebrations. At St Kitts he formally opened the Prince of Wales Bastion. Aboard ship he took part in salvage work and aircraft carrier operations. While *Minerva* was visiting Bermuda he transferred briefly to the survey ship *Fox* to gain further navigational experience and experience of hydrographic work. He qualified for his watch-keeping certificate, his ocean navigation certificate and gained promotion to the rank of lieutenant.

At Easter that year he flew home from the West Indies to join the family gathering at Balmoral which preceded the announcement of Anne's betrothal, after so many earlier denials, to Mark Philips. It was a short trip—and an expensive one. On the day of the announcement he flew from Scotland to Heathrow where, along with his detective and equerry, he boarded a British Airways flight back to the West Indies. The total travel costs for his small party were said to be £1,691.

His tour of duty in the *Minerva* over, he was again in Britain the following November on the occasion of his sister's marriage. It was also, by coincidence, his twenty-fifth birthday. Just after Christmas, following further courses at Portsmouth—a navigation course at HMS *Dryad* and a flight deck officer's course at HMS *Osprey*—he flew out to Singapore to join *Jupiter* as a watch-keeping officer. Then it was off to sea again, to Australia and New Zealand, Fiji, Tonga and Honolulu. He was in the US naval base of San Diego when a telephone call from London brought him news of the attempt to kidnap Princess Anne. After speaking to his sister personally and assuring himself that she was safe and well, though 'shocked and distressed', he decided against flying home and was on deck, saluting and waving, when the frigate pulled out for manoeuvres in the Pacific.

By now he had earned himself a reputation not only as a first-class officer, but, in the words of one of his fellow officers, 'a real character with a sense of humour'. Stories which leaked out later, if they can be believed, showed that he could take a joke as well as make one.

Echoes of the imitation ink blob on mum's carpet in childhood are heard in the story of the doggy-looking object on the floor of the lecture room which caused a deal of nose-wrinkling until Charles, to everyone's astonishment, bent down, scooped it up and popped it back into his document case.

That he could take a joke as well as dish them out is shown by another story of shipboard life. It was the day balloons were being used for target practice. Charles was blowing them up. Someone slipped a contraceptive in amongst them and Charles, so the story goes, had already begun to inflate it before he realized what it was.

Then there was one of those hilarious mess-nights when his fellow officers tried to de-bag him. Grabbing him, they pulled off his trousers—only to find that he was wearing a second pair underneath. A few more seconds and they had those off too—only to be confronted by yet a third pair. After that, they gave up.

That Charles has 'heart' as well as a sense of fun, as his grandmother has said, was shown in Brisbane. He was, at the time, in charge of communications aboard HMS *Jupiter*. A member of the signals staff was unfortunately killed in a road accident while ashore and, in accordance with naval tradition, the dead man's belongings were auctioned off among his shipmates to raise money for his next-of-kin. The total raised on that sad occasion came to a staggering £1500, largely because Charles set the tone of the proceedings by bidding £100 for a rather battered suitcase and even paid £60 for a pair of old socks.

His position as communications officer apparently also enabled him on one occasion to indulge in communications of a sort that were hardly in the line of naval duty. As a result, when *Jupiter* arrived back at Devonport, his fellow-officers discovered that 'Wales' had made good his joking threat to have them all confined to the Tower. Waiting for them on the dockside was a mini-bus which, on Charles' instructions, had been adorned with nine-inch letters labelling it: 'HM Tower of London for Officers of HMS Jupiter'.

Charles was now a fully qualified sea-man officer. A sub-specialist course was the next step in his naval career. He elected to train as a helicopter pilot. Previous flying experience in fixed wing air-craft would be a help and the end-product would also enable him to fly the Wessex Mark 4 helicopters of the Queen's Flight.

Helicopter training saw him posted to 707 Squadron at Royal Naval Air Station Yeovilton in Somerset in September 1974. Almost inevitably, his first trip in a Wessex Mark 5 commando helicopter, with Lieutenant Commander Alan MacGregor, a naval officer serving with the Queen's Flight, as his instructor, resulted in him again being described as 'a natural'. And perhaps he was.

For all that, training was not altogether without incident. There was one occasion when he had to make a forced landing at RAF Benson. A second mid-air emergency was even more alarming. As far as it is possible to piece the story together, Prince Charles was at the controls when a chunk of metal flew off and damaged one of the engines. Flames belched from the exhaust. Calmly, Charles shut down the damaged engine and made a forced landing in a field. When mechanics arrived to fix the damaged engine, he got stuck in and worked alongside them. All work and no play would have made Charles, equally with Jack, a very dull boy indeed, and on the lighter side there was a night out in Okehampton where he saw the sex comedy *Percy's Progress* at the local movie house and then went on to a nearby pub, *The King's Arms,* for a half-pint of that potent West Country drink known as 'scrumpy'.

As part of his training, he landed a Wessex on the deck of the commando carrier *Hermes,* his first solo deck landing, and, to mark the tenth anniversary of 707 Squadron, which coincided with the last week of his course, he led a massed fly-past of naval helicopters. By the end of that week, after a total of 53 hours' ground instruction, 38 hours' dual flying and 15 hours' solo, he was not only a fully qualified helicopter pilot but had won the award for the best pilot on that particular course.

Charles thoroughly enjoyed this new experience of naval flying. He found it, he said, 'very exciting, very rewarding, very stimulating, and sometimes bloody terrifying'.

Judging by the fact that plans for him to take a lieutenants' course at the Royal Naval College, Greenwich, were now temporarily postponed, either the excitement and stimulation outweighed the 'bloody terrifying' moments or, for him, being sometimes terrified was part of the attraction. Whichever it was, the delay in going to Greenwich was at his own request. He wanted to get active experience of flying in a commando support role first.

So he stayed on at Yeovilton for some

advance flying training and also undertook part at least of the rigorous
commando course Royal Marines
undergo at the Lympstone (Devon)
training centre. The idea of an HRH
scaling rope ladders with a blackened
face or swinging hand-over-hand across
a ravine was more than sufficient to
attract the photographers, of course. But
Charles was less easily recognizable on
the commando course than on the parade
ground and one photographer tells an
amusing story of how he walked up to a
chap in camouflage gear and asked,
'When does His Nibs arrive?'

When the man turned, grinning, the
answer was obvious. His Nibs was
already there.

On completion of this further training,
the Prince was assigned to 845 Naval Air
Squadron and in March 1975 he
embarked with the Squadron in the commando ship *Hermes* for a further spell of
sea-going duty in the Western Atlantic
and the West Indies. From the deck of
the *Hermes* he took off on flying stints
which lasted, on one occasion at least, up
to 5½ hours. He was to joke later about

how he risked the danger of contracting haemorrhoids, which is apparently an occupational hazard among those who fly helicopters. Frenzied games of deck hockey afforded exercise during those weeks at sea and there were movies for relaxation. There was also a shore-based spell at Blissville, New Brunswick, a Royal Canadian Air Force base, where he lived rough under canvas for two weeks of sub-zero temperature, and, like his father before him, found it warmer and more convenient to grow a beard.

However, he was again clean-shaven when he finally arrived at Greenwich in the autumn for his three-month course as a junior staff officer. There was a further brief course at HMS *Vernon,* the Navy's mine warfare school at Portsmouth, before journeying north to Rosyth to take command of his first ship. It was hardly the latest, largest or most modern of Britain's fighting ships. On the contrary, it was over twenty years old, built of wood, 153 feet from stem to stern, with a ship's company of four officers and thirty-three ratings, and a skipper's cabin measuring a mere 9 by 8 feet jammed between the ship's refrigerator and the toilets. A minehunter of 360 tons, it was named—appropriately enough, perhaps—after a village in the principality of Wales, HMS *Bronington*.

It was February 1976 when Charles went aboard his new command for the first time. He was now twenty-seven, which was two years younger than his father had been when he took command of the frigate *Magpie* more than a quarter of a century before.

His son's appointment as skipper of the *Bronington* was more than sufficient excuse for Philip to take time out on an official trip to Scotland shortly after in order to pay a nostalgic return visit to Rosyth where he himself was based at one time. Lieutenant His Royal Highness the Prince of Wales accorded Admiral of the Fleet His Royal Highness the Duke of Edinburgh a piped salute as he stepped aboard the minehunter and showed him proudly over the ship before serving him tea and cucumber sandwiches in the diminutive ward-room.

Charles had just returned from an all-night exercise in the Forth estuary and the stubble of a new beard shadowed his chin. A few weeks later, when he sailed *Bronington* into the docks at Barry, Glamorgan, on a three-day visit, the five o'clock shadow had again become what is known in naval circles as 'a full set', giving him a striking resemblance to his dead grandfather, King George VI, in the days when he was a young Duke of York.

But though he may have looked young, Charles didn't feel it. Or so he said.

'I have only been in the Navy five years,' he told Barry's mayor, Reginald Dunkley, 'and sometimes I feel eighty already. I'm sure I have aged about ten years since I took command. I don't know why my beard hasn't turned grey.'

It was doubtless another princely joke.

10   Bachelor

Charles was only four, a bit young for marriage in present-day royal circles whatever may once have been the case, when an enterprising magazine editor published the first short list of eligible young ladies he might one day marry. Most, if not all, of the lisping toddlers in that first-ever list have long since married someone else. However, if at first you don't succeed, try, try, try again. Over the years of his boyhood and teenage the original list was to be extended, amended, endlessly re-ordered as first one girl, then another, became the current top of the matrimonial pops. Denmark's Princess Anne-Marie held the No 1 spot for a long time...until she married Constantine of Greece.

We are perhaps in error in comparing this oft-played journalistic game with the top of the pops. Most editors have preferred to treat it as either a royal Miss

World contest or one of the horse-racing classics, with references to 'favourites' and 'outsiders' and similar betting terms. Throughout the years of his adolescence and young manhood Charles had only to be seen walking, talking, riding, driving, dancing or theatre-going with some delectable young lady for fresh romantic rumours to be sparked and a new name to appear in the charts when the 'Pick Your Next Queen' game was next played. The wonder was that someone didn't patent the idea and market it as a box game. In Britain at least it would probably have outsold Monopoly.

It mattered not where Charles and his latest light-of-love may have been observed or how many other people were around at the time—they could have been cantering round Ascot race course with not less than half-a-dozen others or in the middle of a packed polo crowd at Smith's Lawn—it was sufficient for the girl to be tracked down, identified, friends and relatives interviewed, and for the gossip columnists to assure their readers that this was it, the real thing, the big love in Charles' life.

Take the case of the 'after the show' party he attended while still a schoolboy at Gordonstoun. By show business standards, it was a relatively tame affair, a small matter of tea and cakes rather than champagne drunk from chorus-girls' slippers, given by one of the girls from Elgin Academy who had combined with the Gordonstoun boys for a joint production of *Iolanthe*. Charles was only one of several youngsters from Gordonstoun who attended the gathering, his detective in tow as always. Hardly the circumstances for a romantic *tête-à-tête*. 'It was not a necking party and there was no pairing off,' recalls someone else who was there. 'We were all together in one room.'

Naturally, Charles spoke to others at the party. And naturally, since some of them were girls, some of those he spoke to were girls! One of them was a girl with blonde hair. The very word 'blonde', perhaps because of Anita Loos, would seem to have heady and intriguing connotations. Certainly in this case it was more than sufficient, as soon as Charles left Gordonstoun for Timbertop, for a number of continental magazines to inform their readers that he was being 'exiled' to Australia in order to free him from the romantic clutches of this particular blonde. 'EXILED FOR THE CRIME OF FALLING IN LOVE' was only one of the sillier headlines.

It was all nonsense, of course, as at least one Sunday newspaper in Britain was quick to point out while contriving to repeat all the rumour and gossip at the same time that it denounced it. Even the basic fact around which all the rest of the nonsense was fabricated was untrue. From start to finish most of the publications which joined in this piece of journalistic fun were wrong about even the girl's name. The teenage blonde to whom Charles chatted at the party was not the solicitor's daughter who gave it, as most writers assumed, but another girl entirely, the daughter of a local farmer.

In any event, there was no question of Charles 'chatting her up' in the sense in which that phrase is customarily used today. Other boys of the same age might have done so given the opportunity, but not Charles. Acutely shy as he was at the time, he was a late starter where girls were concerned. At ease though he may have been with them in those more junior days when sister Anne and such other girls as he encountered from time to time, like Mary Beck, daughter of one of his two headmasters at Cheam, were merely playmates, his attitude towards them changed to one of nervousness and apprehension once he was of an age to understand that girls were not simply boys with long hair.

Shy and inhibited as he was at this stage of his development, he had little or no inclination to mix with the opposite sex. And Gordonstoun, in any event, afforded few opportunities for doing so. He was blushingly embarrassed by the titters emanating from the school maids if he happened to pass them in the corridors. With the solitary exception of the *Iolanthe* after-the-show party, he preferred to dodge invitations from girls, whether the local ones living around Gordonstoun or the sisters of his schoolfellows, though both categories were eager to meet him. Girls from St Margaret's School, Aberdeen, invading

Gordonstoun one year to act as partners for the school dance, were disappointed to find no sign of Charles. He had elected to spend that particular weekend with his grandmother at Birkhall. Nor did he join the other boys when they slid off to Pete's Caff to chat up the local talent. And though he might listen to tales of their amatory exploits, doubtless more imaginary than real, he hardly ever spoke about such things himself. However, there was apparently one occasion when he did.

Having outgrown the age of marbles and conkers, it was something of a game among the older boys at Gordonstoun to award marks out of ten, according to their juvenile assessment of her face, figure and legs, to any girl they chanced to see. Charles, according to one of his schoolmates, entered into the spirit of things on his return to Gordonstoun at the end of one vacation by boasting that he had seen 'a real smasher' coming out of Harrods—'worth ten out of ten'.

His shyness apart, there were other factors which prevented him from culti-vating the friendship of the opposite sex at this time. In the era when other youngsters were seeking and gaining a considerably increased degree of social freedom, Charles was almost as restricted and hamstrung as his mother had been in her teenage days a generation before. Because he was who he was, he knew—and particularly so after the business of the cherry brandy—that there could be no question of him frequenting coffee bars and discos as other boys of his age did in their endeavour to meet and get to know girls. Probably he didn't even want to. Most of his young life at this time was passed within the almost monastic confines of Gordonstoun and, later, Timbertop. On holiday he was usually at Balmoral or Sandringham, in the bosom of his family. And if ever he went anywhere without the rest of the family there was always a detective tagging along.

On the rare and fleeting occasion when opportunity may have presented itself, there were still the twin barriers of his shyness and his acute awareness of the specialness of his own position to be hurdled. Far too shy and self-conscious to essay an opening gambit himself, he was also excessively embarrassed on those very few occasions when the opposite sex took matters into their own increasingly liberated hands, blushing deeply, for instance, when a gushing American girl had the boldness to kiss him at the same time that she garlanded him with the traditional *lei* when his plane touched down in Hawaii on the way to Timbertop. Staying briefly in Canberra on the next stage of his journey, he may have gone sailing with the daughter of the Governor-General's secretary (though he is unlikely to have suggested it himself), but returning home by way of Mexico at the end of his Australian schooling he was still too shy and inhibited to have anything to do with an elegant bunch of hand-picked Mexican beauties paraded specially for his benefit.

Finally, there were the reporters and gossip writers, always hawk-like alert for the smallest romantic rumour. The daughter of a Norfolk landowner with whom Charles had danced at a country house ball while staying at Sandringham the previous winter wrote to him while he was at Timbertop. Charles wrote back. Word of this harmless and trivial exchange of letters was leaked to the newspapers and immediately the young lady concerned was listed as his latest 'girlfriend'. She was, of course, a girl. She was also, considering the exchange of letters between them, a friend, though hardly a close one. Put the two words together and you come up with 'girlfriend', though she was never that to Charles in the sense in which the phrase is commonly employed. Yet a 'girlfriend', with all its romantic overtones, she remained —at least, according to some newspapers —until she finally married someone else several years later.

Charles was, in the words of a fellow-student, still 'naïve and old-fashioned' about girls when he went to university at the age of eighteen. Perhaps confused also. The relatively puritan nature of his upbringing insisted that girls who slept with boys 'weren't quite nice'. Yet at Cambridge he found himself meeting girls who were apparently very nice indeed, but who were undeniably sleeping with their boyfriends. Even as late as 1969, when he was already twenty and on the verge of his investiture as Prince of Wales, a girl reporter who talked with him at a cocktail party wrote afterwards that he was still 'disturbed' by girls. 'A sweet virgin boy', she christened him.

But he was growing up all the time and, like any other young man, found himself, gradually, more and more attracted to the opposite sex. He began taking them out, though mostly to approved social functions where there were loads of other people or in small theatre-going groups of four or six young people. For the most part, the girls he took out were the daughters of family friends, sisters of student friends or girls he met a Cambridge of whom he knew his parents would approve, like Sibella Dorman, the daughter of Malta's Governor-General, Sir Maurice Dorman.

Like Charles, Sibella was reading history. Like Charles, she was interested in the amateur stage. So friendship developed. Charles took her out to dinner or, at least, asked her to join him at a dinner party to which he had been invited. He

273

would be going there direct from Sandringham, he said, but would take her
back to Cambridge afterwards. He did—
in the travel-stained Land Rover, piled
high with shooting gear, in which he had
driven from Sandringham. 'I'd expected
the MG at very least', Sibella confided in
a friend afterwards.

Charles invited her to his birthday
party and also to the investiture party
aboard the royal yacht. In return, she
included him among the guests for the
occasional small supper party in her
rooms at Newnham and it was on one of
these occasions that Charles, if not over-
staying his welcome, inadvertently trans-
gressed the college rule of the time that
male guests must be gone by eleven
o'clock. It was perhaps twenty minutes
after the witching hour of eleven when he
made his way out past the porter's lodge,
unchallenged if not unnoticed.

All of this aroused comparatively little
interest on the part of the newspapers.
But not when Charles flew out to spend a
sunspot holiday with Sibella in Malta.
Journalistic nostrils quivered, scenting a
real romance at last. A second holiday in

274

Malta, a year later, saw interest soar to fever point. Sibella, mini-skirted and white-gloved, was at the airport to greet him on arrival. They swam and sun-bathed together, with Sibella, on one occasion at least, helping Charles to apply his suntan oil. Newspapers and the reading public alike were sure that this—at last—was it!

It wasn't, of course. In the fullness of time, Sibella, like many another potential Princess of Wales, was to marry someone else.

Charles, at this stage in his life, rarely went out with a girl in anything remotely approaching a romantic twosome. Even if he did, there would invariably be the inevitable detective almost breathing down the backs of the their necks. More usually, and quite deliberately in an attempt to discourage romantic gossip and the resulting headlines, he went out and about as one of a mixed group of several young people. The ploy seldom worked. Reporters had only to identify the particular girl occupying the next seat at the theatre or sitting beside him in the car for the return trip and the newspapers were immediately plugging the story of 'Prince's New Girlfriend'. If, as sometimes happened, all attempts at identification failed, then she became the 'mystery girl' or something similar, which was perhaps even more intriguing...like the 'attractive blonde' who chatted with him while he changed his shirt at a polo game or the 'mini-skirted date' who accompanied him to the theatre on one occasion.

Charles himself, of course, was well cushioned from investigative journalists pursuing the latest 'girlfriend' story. Members of the palace press staff could equally shrug things off with a 'Don't know' or 'No comment', but the girl herself, once she was identified, was more vulnerable. So were her parents, relatives, friends.

Charles himself had something to say on the subject during a television interview in Australia. Judging from his remarks, he saw the resulting publicity as off-putting to some girls, attractive to others.

'It's worse for her than it is for me. I have layers of things to protect me. It does affect the relationship and it can attract the wrong type of girl.'

Only Charles knows who he may have considered to be 'the wrong type of girl'. Certainly there were times when the pressure of publicity has affected his relationship with a particular girl. There was one girl at least, we have been told, who was reluctantly obliged to inform him finally that she would prefer not to see him again because she could no longer stand the strain of the public spotlight.

As he grew from boyhood to manhood it was perhaps inevitable that the question of marriage should continue to be raised at shortening intervals. With the frankness that one has come to associate with him, Charles did not beat about the bush.

'When you marry in my position,' he told one interviewer, 'you are going to marry someone who perhaps one day is going to become Queen. You have got to choose somebody very carefully, I think, who could fulfil this particular role and it has got to be someone pretty special. The one advantage about marrying a princess, for instance, or somebody from a royal family, is that they do know what happens.'

Princesses and somebodies of royal families whom he might marry are hardly likely to be of British birth and Charles was perhaps as eager to avoid critical headlines—BRITISH GIRLS NOT GOOD ENOUGH FOR CHARLES—as to keep his options open when he added quickly: 'The only trouble is that I often feel that I would like to marry somebody English.' *Oh, dear, that didn't sound right for a Prince of Wales.* 'Or Welsh.' *Oh, dear; now he might have upset the Scots.* 'Well, British anyway.'

Neatly done; well handled. It was the 'princess' bit which tickled the public fancy. Far from criticizing him for not buying British, everyone seemed only too anxious to help him make a satisfactory choice. A surprising number of eligible princesses, mostly of German or mid-European backgrounds, were featured in a fresh rash of short lists which were trotted out in double quick time. The thinnest of connections—perhaps a relationship to the Mountbattens or to Princess Alice, Countess of Athlone, or merely to have attended that same wedding in Greece of Constantine and Anne-Marie at which Charles had been one of the twelve young men who took it in turns to hold the bridal crowns—was all that was necessary to become a firm second favourite in the princely marriage stakes. Many of the princesses so listed were from very minor royal families—indeed, hardly royal at all by British standards—but no one seems to have queried how they might be expected to 'know what happens' on state occasions in Britain any more than the daughter of a British-born earl or duke.

So intense was the speculation that Prince Philip, speaking on American television shortly after, was moved to say that he had never specified who his son should marry.

Not even a princess?

To this query, Philip replied: 'You will find that people tend to marry within their own circles...The advantage perhaps is that there is a certain built-in acceptance of the sort of life you are going to lead.'

There was, of course, plenty of good

British stock available at the time to compete with all these foreign princesses. For starters, there were the various eligible young ladies invited to Windsor Castle for Ascot Week and to similar semi-private royal functions elsewhere, among them the Duke of Northumberland's daughters, Lady Caroline Percy and Lady Victoria Percy; the Duke of Grafton's daughter, Lady Henrietta Fitzroy (she had been in Charles' dancing class as a child, one newspaper reminded its readers); the Duke of Westminster's daughters, Lady Jane Grosvenor and Lady Leonora Grosvenor; Lord Astor's daughter, Louise, to name only a few. The latest list of possible runners in the Prince of Wales Matrimonial Stakes, if not the betting prices, was published at frequent intervals under headlines which ranged from the rather flip 'CHARLIE'S DARLINGS' of one tabloid to the more romantic 'WORLD'S MOST ELIGIBLE BACHELOR' approach of one of the women's magazines.

For Charles to be seen with a girl once was sufficient to justify the inclusion of her name in someone's short list. To be seen with her more than once meant promotion to the temporary level of first or second favourite. Sometimes a girl might even creep into the list with no firm assurance that he had ever met her at all. An unexpectedly fancied outsider, for no other reason than that Charles was known to have dined with her parents while on a visit to France, was the daughter of Prince Rainier of Monaco and the American-born Princess Grace.

She was a Catholic and under the Act of Settlement of 1701 no Catholic can become Britain's Queen. Perhaps it was visualized that Caroline, like Hélène d'Orleans when she fell in love with the Duke of Clarence, then second in line to the British throne, might seek to change her religion.*

Charles' name was linked briefly with that of Sir John Russell's daughter, Georgiana, with hardly more reason. He took her along one day to watch him play polo. He was also 'very fond'—or so it was said at the time—of Lord Balneil's

*THE FULL STORY IS TOLD IN OUR BOOK BERTIE AND ALIX

daughter, Bettina Lindsay. After all, had he not taken her to the theatre and then to a concert at the Albert Hall on successive nights? And the furore over the Westminster girl, Leonora, after she had been to his birthday party and he, in turn, had visited her family's home near Chester, became so great that the poor girl was forced into burbling 'Unfounded and untrue; silly' to rumours of an imminent betrothal.

Certainly it did not seem that Charles, apprehensive as he may have been of girls in schooldays, was ever short of attractive feminine companionship...unlike soldiers in the 1st Battalion, the Royal Regiment of Wales, who, when he visited them at Osnabruck as their Colonel-in-Chief, bewailed their inability to make themselves understood to the local *frauleins*. Charles promptly compiled a suitable phrasebook, had it translated into German on his return to Britain and sent it out to the lovesick privates to assist them in their amorous exploits.

In those fast-changing years of the second half of the sixties newspapers were no longer content to treat the question of Charles and the opposite sex with that degree of veiled romanticism one finds in the works of Victorian lady novelists. An overnight rail trip from Balmoral to London in the company of one young lady was followed by the sort of innuendo which would have been unthinkable even a few years before. As so often, the really clever columnists contrived to get the best of both worlds by knocking down the rumours...to do which they had first to set them up, of course. No, said these clever columnists, of course they did not think there was anything untoward involved. (Nor had their readers until they saw it denied in print.) No, they did not think the heir to the throne was in the clutches of an older woman. But what a pity...etcetera, etcetera, etcetera.

There was a time when such nudge-nudge-wink-wink comments would have embarrassed Charles beyond measure. But now nearly twenty-four and a sea-going naval officer, he was mature and male enough to grin philosophically, though doubtless feeling a degree of sympathy for the unfortunate young lady.

Once considerably embarrassed, later irritated, by the constant references to his 'girlfriends', Charles by now had grown to realize that there was only one way to treat the situation and remain sane...as a joke.

'No blonde with me today', he joked with photographers as he got off a train on which he had travelled to Scotland.

'I wonder which of you I will be engaged to tomorrow', he grinned at a crowd of middle-aged mums who had gathered to watch him move off on a grouse shoot.

He had also matured in the sense that he no longer considered it necessary to be cocooned by three, four or five other young people whenever he went out with a girl. Like any other young man, he would now make a date over the telephone, collect the girl of the moment in his own car and whip her off on her own to a theatre or restaurant. Well, perhaps not quite like any other young man of his age. A watchful detective, you can be sure, was never very far away.

Of all the romantic rumours which

dogged Charles over the years, the most persistent was that linking his name with Lady Jane Wellesley, daughter of the Duke of Wellington.

The gossip, as nearly as one can pin-point such things, started in the late summer of 1973, with Charles nearing his twenty-fifth birthday. 'Idiotic', said the Duke of Wellington when a Sunday newspaper reported that Charles and Jane would be betrothed by the end of the year. 'Pure fabrication', added the Duchess.

However, the original rumour was not only fired afresh but given a new degree of credibility when Charles, in the same month that Princess Anne married Mark Phillips, spent a holiday with Jane on the 3000-acre Wellington estate of Molmo de Ray in romantic Grenada. Anne's be-trothal to Mark Phillips had been an-nounced only after a succession of denials which had deceived no one but left a decided distaste for official and semi-official royal statements in several journalistic mouths. It was perhaps knowledge of this fact which caused the Prince's personal detective, in rejecting a request that Charles and Jane should pose together for photographs, to say: 'The Prince will not be a party to deception. That is why he has declined to be photographed with Lady Jane.'

Making a statement that was presumably authorized by Charles himself, Inspector Paul Officer went on, 'The whole affair has been built up from a molehill into a mountain. I can definitely state that there is no romance.' Aware of the interpretation which the gossip columnists these days attach to the old Hollywood 'just good friends' cliché, Inspector Officer contrived to avoid it. But only just. 'They are just *very good chums.'**

After all the Anne and Mark subterfuge and denials—or perhaps it would have been the same if that had never happened—the newspapers were prepared to take nothing on trust and Sandringham found itself under siege by reporters and photographers when Charles and Jane went there for the New Year. An unnamed villager suddenly became an

*OUR ITALICS

authority on royal marriage. 'From what I have overheard between members of the royal circle, there is definitely something in it', he was quoted as saying.

Speculation such as this was calculated to fuel public interest and on the Sunday, when the royal party, including Charles and Jane, attended morning service in the parish church, crowds of eager-beaver sightseers, attracted by what they had read in the weekend newspapers as mice are attracted by toasted cheese, converged on Sandringham from all parts of East Anglia and the Midlands. Despite a Government plea to save petrol because of the current oil crisis, the car park was already filled to overflowing a full hour and a half before the church service was due to commence and motorists arriving after that, some of whom were making a 100-mile round trip or more to be there, were compelled to park their cars anything up to two miles away and hoof the rest. By the time the service ended and the royal party left church there was a crowd which Charles himself later estimated at some 10,000 people.

In a subsequent speech to the Parliamentary Press Gallery, during which he cautioned newspapers and television against confusing freedom with licence, he harked back to that Sunday morning crowd. 'Such was the obvious conviction that what they had read was true that I almost felt I had better espouse myself at once so as not to disappoint so many people.

'As you can see, I thought better of it.'

But that statement came only at the end of eighteen months during which Lady Jane continued to be No 1 favourite for the Princess of Wales Stakes, the odds even shortening somewhat when she accompanied the Queen Mother and Princess Alexandra to the 1974 Royal Film Performance, a sure sign, it was said with many a nudge and wink, that she was being gently groomed for higher things. The odds on her lengthened again, however, when a shapely young American named Laura Jo Watkins, the daughter of Rear Admiral James Watkins, flew all the way to London to be in the distinguished visitors' gallery when the heir to the throne made his maiden speech to the House of Lords.

Charles had met Laura Jo while serving aboard HMS *Jupiter*. The ship had docked at San Diego and Charles had gone along to a cocktail party given by the British Consul. Laura Jo was also there and they had a chat about surfing. This seemingly not-very-romantic conversation took place, as one newspaper reported with bated breath, 'just a mile from where a previous Prince of Wales first met Mrs Simpson'.

Speculation that an Anglo-American romance was again in the offing hardened when sharp-eyed reporters spotted that Laura Jo, as she sat in the distinguished visitors' gallery at the House of Lords, was wearing a pearl ring on the third finger left hand. Could it be that the Prince and the shapely American were already engaged? And what about that mysterious business of the function at London's US Embassy which Charles had been unable to attend because the Royals were in mourning for his great-uncle, the Duke of Gloucester? Laura Jo was there, but only for a short time. Then she disappeared. Had she been whisked away to Buck House? Once again it was necessary for someone to deny that there was anything at all romantic in all this. Any such speculation was '180 degrees out', said a spokesman for the Watkins family.

But the newspaper gossip and speculation had the inevitable effect and there was a larger-than-usual crowd at Cowdray Park that weekend, neck craning to see who Charles might have with him, when he arrived there to play polo. To everyone's obvious disappointment, Laura Jo was not in tow. Someone had the temerity to ask where she was.

'You don't think I'm such a bloody fool as to bring her here today,' Charles chortled.

By the following month, with shapely Laura Jo back home in California, Lady Jane was again firm favourite. Convinced that a betrothal announcement was finally imminent, some three hundred photographers and reporters converged on Strathfield Saye, Berkshire home of the Duke and Duchess of Wellington, when the Queen and Philip went there to take a look at the annual Game Fair of the County Land-

Making her first public appearance with her future husband, Lady Diana wears a strapless evening gown in black silk taffeta

Already secretly engaged, Lady Diana climbs into her Mini Metro to drive to Buckingham Palace. The engagement was officially announced the following day

Lady Diana meets some of the village folk of Tetbury who will be her neighbours in Gloucestershire

Prince Charles and Lady Diana at the première of the James
Bond film *For Your Eyes Only*

Together at Royal Ascot where Lady Diana was a hit with
her hats

Above left: As patron of the International Year of the Disabled, Prince Charles visits Worcester College for the Blind. *Above right:* Well wrapped against the elements, a 'pining' Prince Charles watches a rescue demonstration while visiting New Zealand

Prince Charles and his mount part company during the Grand Military Gold Cup at Sandown

Right: Prince Charles and Lady Diana visit Cheltenham police headquarters. Police from here will safeguard their home at Highgrove

Below: With their wedding only a week or so away, Prince Charles and Lady Diana relax together at Windsor

Charles and his brotherly supporters, Prince Andrew and Prince Edward, at the start of the wedding ceremony

A fairy-tale bride and bridegroom leave St Paul's Cathedral after the wedding

The newly-married Prince and Princess of Wales drive to Buckingham Palace through cheering thousands

On the palace balcony after the wedding. With the newlyweds are *(left to right)* Catherine Cameron, Lady Sarah Armstrong-Jones and Lord Nicholas Windsor

The newlyweds, smiling happily, drive to Waterloo station at the start of their honeymoon

owners' Association. To the disappointment of one and all, no such announcement was forthcoming.

It is easy, of course, to be wise after the event, but the fact remains that Charles, at that time, had no thoughts of marriage and no intention of getting hitched for at least some years to come. He was enjoying his sea-going and bachelor way of life too much to want to settle down. He may not exactly have had the sailor's traditional girl-in-every-port, but there were few ports of call where he did not quickly find an attractive partner to talk to, dine with, dance with. When the *Hermes* was in Montreal, for instance, he went disco dancing with a receptionist from the British embassy— and was flatly turned down by a Canadian girl whom he also asked for a dance. She was too tired, she told him, and was going home. Even a prince can't win them all, it seems.

The summer of 1976 found a new name heading the list of matrimonial favourites. Some two years before, Davina Sheffield, a cousin of Lord McGowan, had visited Balmoral with the result that she had been included in the list of possible brides published by more than one newspaper. Then she had dropped out of the limelight when she went to Vietnam to undertake relief work. Back in Britain, escorted to Smith's Lawn by Charles on a weekend when he had excused himself from attending the Swedish wedding of King Carl Gustav on the grounds of pressure of work, sitting with the Queen and Prince Philip to watch the polo and leaving again with Charles in his Aston Martin at the end of the day, she suddenly found herself—in the eyes of the gossip columnists, at least—the firmest of firm favourites. Subsequently she and Charles were rumoured to have holidayed secretly together in Devon and unnamed friends went on record as predicting that the couple would certainly marry 'next year.' As things turned out, however, there was to be no marriage between Charles and Davina 'next year' or any other year.

Twice—in 1977 and again in 1980—Buckingham Palace found it necessary to deny rumours that Charles was to be betrothed to Princess Marie-Astrid of Luxembourg. For all that Marie-Astrid's parents are longtime friends of Charles' parents, a royal marriage alliance was never contemplated. Nor could it have been without changing the Act of Settlement which bars the heir to the throne from marrying a Catholic. In any event, Charles and Marie-Astrid themselves had hardly met.

Another name which cropped up in the Princely Matrimonial Stakes at more or less regular intervals was that of Amanda Knatchbull, daughter of Lord Brabourne, granddaughter of Earl Mountbatten of Burma. Nothing would have delighted Mountbatten more, it was hinted in the gossip columns, than for his granddaughter and great-nephew to wed. Charles had only to see his Knatchbull cousin on holiday for gossip column speculation to harden and royal spokesmen to trot out a weary insistence that 'they were simply old family friends'.

Just as the Knatchbulls are 'old family friends', so are the Spencers. Earl Spencer himself may have had little contact with the Royal Family since he and his first wife divorced, but Charles himself did not see the divorce as any reason why he should not befriend the eldest of the three Spencer daughters, Sarah, in the aftermath of her spell of ill-health. He provided cheerful companionship, riding with her, taking her to polo games, going on a skiing holiday with her and inviting her to stay with his family at Sandringham. In return, she invited him for a weekend visit to her home, Althorp Hall.

It was at Althorp that weekend, in the middle of a ploughed field, that he first met the younger sister he was destined to marry. Looking at him through the eyes of the sixteen-year-old schoolgirl she then was, she appears to have thought him 'pretty amazing'. For his part, Charles thought no more than that she was 'very jolly, amusing, great fun, bouncing and full of life'.

At the time it was Sarah who was kept busy denying she was in love with Charles. 'He makes me laugh,' she was quoted as saying in an interview published in February, 1978. He seems like the big brother I've never had. He's fabulous, but I am not in love with him. There is no question of me being the future Queen of England. I don't think he's met her yet.'

In that, of course, she was wrong. Charles had already met the future Queen of England even if he himself was equally unaware of the fact. Not for another three years, during which time that amusing sixteen-year-old matured into an attractive nineteen-year-old, would he see her with fresh eyes. In the meantime there were to be other girls... old friends like Jane Wellesley, new favourites like Sabrina Guinness and Anna Wallace. Perhaps Sarah Spencer (as she was then) hit the nail on the head when she said, in the course of another interview, 'Prince Charles is a romantic who falls in love easily.'

Easily, perhaps, but not permanently —until the late summer of 1980 when, at Balmoral, he met up with Diana again.

11 Suitor

It is a long-standing royal tradition to spend each summer at Balmoral Castle, that cross between a chieftain's fortress and a Rhineland *schloss* which Prince Albert devised for Queen Victoria. The summer of 1980 found the Royals there as usual, Prince Charles as well as his parents...which presented fate with an opportunity to give a new twist to the old 'Spot the Bride' game.

The chores of royal life go on even during holidays, and so the Queen always has one of her private secretaries along with her. And to give everyone a fair crack of the whip, there is usually a changeover at around the halfway stage of the royal stay. Even so, Robert Fellowes, the assistant private secretary whose turn it was at this particular time, had his wife Jane with him for company. Jane is the second of Earl Spencer's three daughters and what more natural than that Diana, on holiday herself, should also journey north to help her sister with her first baby.

The sixteen-year-old schoolgirl Charles had first met on his visit to Althorp Hall as sister Sarah's guest some three years earlier was now a young woman of nineteen, still as amusing and full of fun as ever, but now tall and attractive with it, delightful feminine companionship for those fishing and shooting excursions which feature so largely in the royal holiday programme at Balmoral. Charles, as he walked and talked with her, discovered that the two of them had much in common...mutual interests such as music and skiing, the same love of country life and, perhaps most important of all, the same sort of sense of humour. It did not take him long to realize that here, at last, after so many girlfriends, flirtations, romances, was the one girl who combined all the qualities to make him an ideal wife and serve the country as a future Queen.

He spoke of his feelings for Diana to his grandmother, the Queen Mother, to whom he has always been so close. She could not have been more delighted. Diana's grandmother, Ruth, Lady Fermoy, had long been one of her closest friends as well as her lady-in-waiting. Eagerly she entered into a conspiracy to give young love a chance of establishing itself without interference from the newspapers and later that year, with Charles again visiting Balmoral, Diana stayed with the Queen Mother at nearby Birkhall. 'The whole thing was planned like a military operation,' Charles recalls.

Their romance could not remain a secret for long, of course, but long enough for them to examine, test and become certain of their feelings for each other. Then, with Diana's return to London, the newspapers were soon full of 'the new girl in the life of Prince Charles', with reporters and photographers laying siege to her flat and the kindergarten where she worked. It was a very considerable ordeal for a sensitive girl of nineteen and the wonder was that she did not cut and run, as at least one other young lady is said to have done before her.

From time to time there has been talk of potential brides and grooms being invited to Balmoral (and/or Sandringham) to test their suitability or otherwise for marriage into the Royal Family. There are, these days, no such 'tests', whatever may have been the case in Queen Victoria's day. Having married for love herself, the Queen is perfectly happy for her children to do the same. But if there was never any test of this sort for Diana, the persistence of the reporters and photographers who trailed her here, there and everywhere, the ever-clicking cameras and the intrusive questions assuredly tested her in much sterner fashion. She survived the ordeal well, keeping both her composure and her sense of humour, displaying considerable diplomacy and tact. More than that, some understanding of what she was going through gained her a deal of sympathy among those who read what was written in the newspapers and even among some of the very reporters whose attentions she found so harassing at times.

Only once did she slip up, unwittingly

permitting herself to be manoeuvred into a pose which resulted in her legs being revealed through her dress in the published photograph. She was embarrassed beyond measure, but Charles, it seems, was understanding about it all, slightly amused even and thought her legs looked fine.

Like Anne and Mark before them, at this delicate, still uncertain stage of their relationship, they did their best to avoid being seen together in public. But they would have been less than human for her not to have been there when he rode in a three-mile steeplechase at Ludlow. It was the first time he had ridden his horse, Allibar, in an actual race and he was not too displeased at finishing second. Diana was so thrilled that she jumped for joy and not only because she had backed him each way.

Harassment from the newspapers continued. If Diana herself took it without complaint, others waxed indignant on her behalf. Her mother, the Hon. Mrs Shand-Kydd since her divorce and re-marriage, wrote to *The Times:* 'May I ask the editors of Fleet Street whether, in the execution of their jobs, they consider it necessary or fair to harass my daughter daily from dawn until well after dusk.' Even the Queen was moved to spring to the defence of her prospective daughter-in-law after a Sunday newspaper printed a story alleging a secret late-night meeting between Charles and Diana aboard the royal train. She authorized the palace Press Office to deny the story 'on the authority of the Queen' and the denial was reinforced with a letter to the newspaper saying that 'grave exception' had been taken to the story. Charles followed his mother's denial with one of his own and Diana added hers. She was in London, not Wiltshire, on the night in question, she said.

It was the biggest of a number of hiccups in palace-press relations as the royal romance ran its course, with the newspapers seeking to hurry things along and the Royals endeavouring to protect the reputation of the girl who, it seemed more and more probable, would one day be Queen. Prince Charles showed something of what he was feeling when reporters and photographers besieged Sandringham over the New Year expecting Diana to be there. 'May I take this opportunity to wish you all a very happy New Year', he said to one group of pressmen he encountered, 'and your editors a particularly nasty one.'

In fact, Diana was not at Sandringham to see in the New Year. She might have been, but she was laid low with 'flu over Christmas. However, she had been there earlier, for the weekend following Charles' thirty-second birthday, and she was briefly there again later in January. Then, in February, suddenly and mysteriously she vanished. She had gone to Australia. That much the newspapers were able to establish. But not all the resources of Fleet Street could succeed in tracking her down in that vast expanse. She had gone 'to have a good think about her future', one newspaper guessed.

In fact, her future, when she flew out to Australia for an away-from-it-all holiday in readiness for what lay ahead, had already been decided. Charles had already asked her to marry him. 'I wanted to give her a chance to think about it,' he revealed later. But Diana

302

was sure of her feelings and needed no time for reflection. She accepted him on the spot.

While she was away in Australia, Charles did the right thing. He contacted his future father-in-law, Earl Spencer, and asked for his daughter's hand in marriage. 'I don't know what he would have said if I had turned him down,' the Earl joked.

Of course he did no such thing. What father would? Charles also journeyed again to Sandringham to tell his parents that he had proposed and been accepted. At the age of thirty-two, it was perhaps hardly necessary for him to seek parental permission. But as a descendant of George II and heir to the throne, he needed the Queen's formal consent, not as his mother but as the reigning Sovereign, before he could marry. She was only too happy to give it.

The prospect of so young a daughter-in-law and of further grandchildren in the direct line of succession to the throne delighted her. There was a time when the fact that the bride's parents had divorced and re-married—her mother was now the

Hon. Mrs Frances Shand-Kydd while her father had married Barbara Cartland's daughter, the former Countess of Dartmouth—might have ruled her out as a wife for the Prince of Wales and the role of Britain's future Queen. But in an era when the Queen's sister, Princess Margaret, had herself been through the divorce courts, that no longer mattered.

Returning from her holiday in Australia, Diana was already being treated as the future Queen even if hardly any of those involved had the slightest idea why such preferential treatment was being accorded. She was enabled to bypass the usual customs check at London airport and was smuggled out through a security gate. Later that week she accompanied Charles on a visit to Nick Gaselee's stables in Berkshire when he took his racehorse Allibar out for a morning canter in preparation for another steeplechase in which he had entered. He was on his way back to the stables when the horse suddenly stumbled and sank to its knees. Charles managed to slip out of the saddle just in time as Allibar collapsed completely, rolled over and died from what proved to be a heart attack. Charles knelt at the side of the horse, extremely distressed, and, according to one observer, wept as the animal died. It is not improbable. He is a young man of considerable sensitivity and tenderness. Diana too had 'tears running down her cheeks' as she realized what had happened.

But the shock of Allibar's death was eased by the excitement of the next few days. Two days later, on Sunday, Charles gave Diana her engagement ring, a large oval sapphire surrounded by sixteen diamonds in a setting of white gold. A few people had already been let in on the secret of their betrothal—his parents, hers, their grandmothers, her two sisters, the three girls who shared the flat she would no longer need—and on Tuesday, February 24, the rest of the world was given the news. 'It is with the greatest of pleasure', said an announcement issued from Buckingham Palace, 'that the Queen and the Duke of Edinburgh announce the betrothal of their beloved son, the Prince of Wales, to Lady Diana Spencer, daughter of the

Earl of Spencer and the Honourable Mrs Shand-Kydd.'

More than any other member of the Royal Family, Charles has long taken full advantage of what is known as 'the media'. So it came as no very great surprise to find television cameras in his private sitting-room at the palace on the day of his betrothal. Holding hands, he and a somewhat shyer, though radiant, Diana discussed the past, present and future of their relationship for the benefit of televiewers and newspaper readers around the world.

Their first meeting. 'In the middle of a ploughed field,' said Diana.

Courtship. 'Planned like a military operation,' said Charles.

The proposal. Charles again. 'I wanted to give her a chance to think about it—to think if it was all going to be too awful.' Diana: 'I never had any doubts.'

Shared interests. Charles: 'Love of outdoors. Skiing.' Diana: 'Music and dancing, and we both have the same sense of humour.' But she did not ride, she confessed. 'I fell off a horse and lost my nerve.' Charles (in an aside): 'We'll remedy that.'

The age gap. Diana: 'I haven't really thought about it.' Charles: 'It's only twelve years. Diana will help me to stay young.'

Their future home. Highgrove in Gloucestershire would be their main base, Charles said. 'We've only got one room decorated downstairs and the bedroom organized. Otherwise everything is being painted. There's nothing there yet —no curtains, carpets, furniture.'

Her future as Princess of Wales. Charles: 'She will be twenty soon and I was about that age when I started. It's difficult to start with, but you just have to plunge in.' Diana: 'With Charles beside me, it can't go wrong.'

And were they in love? 'Of course,' said Diana.

12 Prince and Princess

When Charles married Lady Diana Spencer in St Paul's Cathedral on 29th July 1981, he was the first heir to the throne to take an English bride for something over three centuries. The last to do so before him was the prince—though not Prince of Wales—who became King James II and was ultimately chased out of the country. He married Lady Anne Hyde, daughter of the Earl of Clarendon, though she did not live long enough to become queen.

The Hanoverian Georges who followed all married German princesses, as did William IV. Mary II had been married to a Dutchman, William of Orange, and her sister, Queen Anne, married Prince George of Denmark. Queen Victoria, who followed William IV on to the throne, married Albert of Saxe-Coburg, another German. Their eldest son, the Prince of Wales who

308

became Edward VII, married a Danish princess, Alexandra. George V married Mary of Teck, daughter of a German duke. The Queen Mother, though born in England, is the daughter of a Scottish earl. In any event, the Duke of York, as King George VI was at the time of their marriage, was not then heir to the throne; the heir was his eldest brother, the then Prince of Wales.

And if it was three centuries since an heir to the throne took an English bride, it was a great deal longer—480 years—since one had married in St Paul's. The last time that happened was in 1501 when Arthur Tudor, Prince of Wales and elder brother of the future Henry VIII, married the unfortunate Catherine of Aragon in the old St Paul's which was later to go up in flames in the Great Fire of London.

So the choice of St Paul's for the royal wedding represented a surprise departure from recent precedence. Prior to the present century members of the Royal Family had mostly married in the private chapels attached to royal palaces. Princess Patricia, daughter of the Duke of

Connaught and granddaughter of Queen Victoria, started the new trend for Westminster Abbey when she married there soon after the end of World War I. The Queen Mother was married there only a few years later. The Queen, her sister, Princess Margaret, her cousin, Princess Alexandra, and her daughter, Princess Anne, were all married there in turn.

The decision to switch to St Paul's was Charles' 'personal choice', said a Buckingham Palace statement, 'and that of Lady Diana.' An important consideration was the fact that St Paul's could hold several hundred more wedding guests than the Abbey.

If the Abbey authorities were disappointed, those of the Cathedral were correspondingly delighted. The BBC, planning the biggest royal television spectacular of all time, was equally delighted. 'It's a longer route,' Cliff Morgan, head of outside broadcasts, pointed out enthusiastically, 'and we have that lovely sweep up Ludgate Hill and round into the Cathedral.'

Perhaps more than any other member of the Royal Family, Charles is both aware of the importance of television in sustaining the royal image and prepared to play along with it. He has been described more than once as 'a TV natural'. Certainly he has never been frightened of the medium as his parents—even father Philip—were the first time they faced up to it. Honesty requires the admission that the Queen was frankly terrified the first time she appeared on television, in Canada, and hardly more at ease the following Christmas when she made her first Christmas telecast from Sandringham. Even Philip, on his first-ever appearance, was so nervous that his hands shook. But not Charles. Even his earliest interviews—on radio with Jack de Manio; on television with Cliff Michelmore and Brian Connell—he really enjoyed.

'I wasn't really nervous...I like acting and I enjoy imitating...If you happen to have a good television personality, then it is obviously worth utilizing that gift.'

Charles has utilized not only that particular gift, but others, the ability to crack a good joke, the talent to write a speech, script or magazine article. On television he has not been content merely to be interviewed. He devised and directed one sequence of the BBC film dealing with his naval career; and he wrote at least part of the script for his conducted television tour of Canterbury Cathedral. Following his investiture as Prince of Wales, he even turned television reporter for a couple of days, flitting around his principality by helicopter while putting together a rural documentary called *Countryside 70*.

At one stopping place he squatted on a log to chat with a seventy-five-year-old farmer named Dafydd Edwardes. Mr Edwardes, it appeared, did not hold with artificial insemination. Charles seemed inclined to agree with him, though perhaps for different reasons.

'It's unfair on the rams and bulls,' he quipped. 'They get terrible psychological problems, I'm told.'

That same year, wearing a red robe trimmed with the four bands of ermine which are the hallmark of a duke, all part of another quaint old British ceremony, he took his seat in the House of Lords. He was sponsored by the Duke of Kent and the Duke of Beaufort. The occasion was witnessed by several of his relatives. Earl Mountbatten of Burma and the Earl of Snowdon, who are also members of that august but controversial body which left-wing politicians think has outlived whatever usefulness it once had, watched from their own seats. Princess Anne, Princess Margaret and Princess Alexandra looked down from the gallery. But there was no affectionate glance, as there had been at his investiture as Prince of Wales, from his mother. As Queen, she was not permitted to be there.

'In company with convicts, lunatics and peers of the realm, I am ineligible to vote', Charles was to tell Australians later.

But he was free to speak in the House of Lords, though it was to be another four years before he made his maiden delivery.

Like his father, Charles prefers to write his own speeches. Even that 1975 luncheon speech to the Water Rats, despite its references to tracking down a suitable ghost-writer, was all his own work, Buckingham Palace has assured

313

us. The ghost-writer references were 'only a joke', it seems.

Charles was not quite twenty-one when his great-uncle, Mountbatten of Burma, invited him to address the Gandhi Centenary celebrations in London's Albert Hall. Charles being so young, it might be advisable, thought Uncle Dickie, to rough out a suitable speech for him to deliver. He did so and passed it to Charles to read. To his surprise, Charles, after reading it, passed it back.

'I wonder if you'd mind terribly if I didn't use this,' he said as diplomatically as possible. 'I'll write my own and show it to you for your comments.'

He has gone on writing his own speeches ever since, some good, some not so good. Set down in print, that first-ever speech to the Lords hardly reads as the sort of stuff calculated to set the Thames on fire. Probably it sounded better in the flesh. Certainly Lord Shepherd the Lord Privy Seal, was to refer to it as 'a notable maiden speech'.

It was the first time in ninety years that an heir to the throne had spoken from the floor of the House. The last one to do so was Charles' great-great-grandfather Edward VII, in the days when he was Prince of Wales.

As nearly always, Charles had a joke to get started—about three royal dukes who took part in a debate back in 1829 and used such language to each other that the remainder of the noble Lords were shocked into horrified silence. That, Charles promised, would not happen between him and his cousin, Kent.

It was a sports and leisure debate, with Charles speaking in support of a recommendation to set up urban parks and recreation areas. He quoted from Aristotle, the Greville memoirs, Oscar Wilde, an unnamed Doctor of Philosophy at Yale University and his father, Prince Philip. Perhaps the only truly original idea in the speech was that recreational facilities at schools are wasted by virtue of the fact that schools are closed down for so much of the year. And even that may have been said by someone before him. It has a slightly familiar ring.

He criticized the lack of co-ordination

in the whole area of sports and leisure. 'As is so often the case in Britain, an astonishing number of societies, clubs and other bodies of all sorts spring up to deal with the same problem. An element of co-ordination is essential if their efforts are not to be wasted and resources squandered.'

A second speech in the Lords the following year read rather better. This time the topic under debate was voluntary service in the community, with Charles particularly careful to avoid the mistake his father had made at almost the beginning of his career as a professional prince when a too-honest utterance caused him to be labelled 'a royal meddler'.

Royalty may believe privately that conscription is good for the soul; even desirable for the defence of the nation. It did not pay, even in Philip's young days, to say so. And, in today's Britain, you can be sure that Charles would have been called something more than 'a meddler' had he dared reiterate his father's remark.

He didn't. On the contrary, he was at some pains to make it clear that he could see no reasonable or logical justification for re-introducing National Service. But based on his experience at Gordonstoun, he also felt that there should be some way of re-creating the challenges of war in a peacetime environment so that adolescents in particular could discover themselves and their capabilities in the face of hardship and adventure.

'It seems to me,' the Prince told the Lords, 'that the problems we suffer in society through violence and anti-social behaviour on the part of some young people are partly due to a lack of outlets in which their energy, frustration and desire for adventure can be properly channelled.'

If Charles had hoped that he might be left in peace to concentrate on his university studies once investiture as Prince of Wales was over and done with, he was doomed to disappointment. The months ahead were to be even more punctuated by royal chores than those which had gone before. There was to be much more foreign travel,* though this, for someone

*APPENDIX IV

who enjoys travel as much as Charles does, is perhaps a pleasure as well as a chore.

To mark European Conservation Year,* he set up a committee, with himself as chairman, designed to prod his Welsh principality into a greater awareness of the richness of its national heritage. His *Countryside 70* television documentary had the same aim in view. It was as chairman of this committee that he journeyed to Strasbourg, in company of his father, to attend the Council for Europe's Conservation Conference.

During the spring vacation, while other undergraduates were cramming for their forthcoming examinations, he flew out to New Zealand to join his parents and sister for a royal tour 'down under'. He took his books with him, but had little time even to look at them. From New Zealand he went to Japan for Expo 70. In Japan, among other things, he sampled raw fish as part of a traditional Japanese lunch (in the Canadian Arctic he was later to sample raw seal liver also)

*1970

and had his back and shoulders massaged by a Geisha girl. At least, these
were the things which got the publicity.
What went unpublicized at the time was
the fact that he also met the chairman of
a large Japanese electronics concern to
whom he said, 'Have you ever thought of
opening a factory in Wales?' That
particular Japanese concern now has a
factory in South Wales, which goes to
show that the Royals are something very
much more than merely a collection of
pretty faces.

Japan was followed by a tour of
Canada. In Yellowknife he went to what
was perhaps one of the most unroyal
functions ever, a barbecue for young
people, most of whom, if they were not
actually hippies, seemed to favour the
hippy way of dress and a hippy lifestyle.
The barbecue area was heavily littered
with discarded cartons and empty
bottles. Even so, Charles was taken
aback when one youngster spoke to him
in the bluntest fashion he had experienced since that pre-investiture visit to
Cardiff.

'What's so special about you?' he demanded rudely, almost aggressively. 'You seem to get all the publicity.'

Startled though he was initially by this verbal onslaught, Charles recovered sufficiently to retort: 'Don't ask me. Ask the press.'

From Canada he and Anne went on, minus their parents, for a three-day visit to Washington as guests of the Nixons. It was theoretically a private visit, but Mr Nixon, never one to miss an opportunity for burnishing the presidential image, had a fanfare of trumpets and a military band playing *Rule Britannia* to greet the young Royals on their arrival. By way of entertainment, there was another barbecue (a much more sedate one at Fort David), a baseball game to watch, and a ball to which Charles escorted the Nixons' elder daughter, Tricia.

For Charles, the visit passed off remarkably well. A wire service report summed him up as 'charming, sexy and adroit', adding that 'if he weren't in line to be King of England, he might be able to catch on fast in politics over here'. Anne, at least with members of the women's press corps, proved rather less popular.

October of that same year found Charles in Fiji, representing his mother at the island's independence celebrations. Always busy, he wrote his review of the Secombe book for *Punch* on the plane out. He went on to visit the Gilbert and Ellice Islands, Bermuda (for the 350th anniversary of the island's Parliament) and Barbados.

There was one more overseas trip before the year ended, to Paris, to represent the Queen at the memorial service for General de Gaulle.

His naval career was subsequently to be not infrequently interrupted, as studies at Cambridge had been, by the call of royal duty. In 1973, for instance, while serving on the frigate *Minerva*, he opened the newly-restored Prince of Wales Bastion on St Kitts and visited the Bahamas as his mother's special representative at the independence celebrations there.

That autumn, alongside taking a navigational course at HMS *Dryad*, the Navy's shore establishment at Portsmouth, and a flight deck course at HMS

Osprey, Charles attended his sister's wedding, marking the occasion with a diamond brooch for her and a pair of gun cases for the bridegroom; accompanied his mother to the annual opening of Parliament; journeyed to Chester to receive the Freedom of the City, to Bristol where he was made a member of the Society of Merchant Venturers, to Launceston to lunch with tenants of his Duchy of Cornwall estate and to the Welsh Depot at Crickhowell, where he presented new colours to the 3rd battalion, the Royal Regiment of Wales, of which he is Colonel-in-Chief.

By then it was time to fly out to Singapore to join HMS *Jupiter*. Hardly was he aboard than the frigate, by what can hardly have been coincidence, found itself at Lyttleton, New Zealand, at exactly the same time that his mother was there on the royal yacht *Britannia*. Anne and Mark were along too, enjoying what was perhaps in the nature of a second honeymoon. Philip had gone on ahead to open the Commonwealth Games in Christchurch. 'A family gathering', the Queen called it, and so it was. Charles saw his mother open Parliament as Queen of New Zealand and watched the historic pageant which was mounted to mark New Zealand Day. During a visit to a sheep station near Masterton he tried his hand at sheep dipping, this time, we are delighted to record, without falling in. As a small boy, trying to help out on one occasion when sheep were being dipped at Windsor, he overbalanced, fell in and was hauled out dripping with smelly dye.

Naval work and royal duties continued to go hand in hand. When *Jupiter* called at the American naval base of San Diego prior to manoeuvres in the Pacific, Charles found himself lumbered with a busy round of goodwill calls. He visited the Walter Annenbergs at their home in Palm Springs, met Ronald Reagan, then Californian Governor, and his wife and shared a mug of tea with Barbra Streisand during a visit to a film studio.

That September, coincident with his helicopter conversion course, he found himself flying out to New Zealand to attend the funeral of Mr Norman Kirk. The following month he represented the Queen at the centenary celebrations in

Fiji before travelling on to Australia to inaugurate the Anglo-Australian telescope at Siding Spring. He crammed in visits to several other places, including Tasmania, at the same time. He visited the old gold rush towns of Bendigo and Ballarat—'I trust you won't waste good drinking time once I've gone into the town hall,' he told those who turned out to see him in Bendigo—and visited his old school, the Geelong Church of England Grammar School. He watched a surf carnival at Coolangatta on the Queensland coast and was astonished to find himself being watched by a crowd of some 2000 people when he ventured out for an early-morning dip.

Addressing a joint session of the New South Wales Parliament in Sydney, he expressed his firm belief that 'the institution of monarchy to which, rightly or wrongly, I belong and which I represent to the best of my ability, is one of the strongest factors in the continuance of a stable government.'

In February 1975, prior to joining the *Hermes,* came a trip to Katmandu for the coronation of King Birendra of Nepal.

Great-uncle Dickie accompanied him and they stopped off *en route* in New Delhi where Mountbatten showed him round the palace he had occupied as Viceroy in the declining days of the British Raj and, briefly, as Governor-General in the early days of independence. There was also lunch with Mrs Gandhi and a polo game on the Jaipur ground where the late Duke of Windsor also played when he was Prince of Wales in the 1920s. Charles' team won by nine goals to six, with Charles himself scoring two of the goals.

Then it was on to Nepal for the coronation ceremony. Watching, Charles must have been heartily glad that his own coronation in the distant future will take place in London and not in Katmandu. For a start, the ceremony took place at 8.37 a.m. precisely because the local royal astrologers had decided on that as the most propitious time. And while King Charles III will merely be anointed with holy oil, poor King Birendra had to submit to being smeared with holy mud collected from suitably symbolic places —a Himalayan peak, the bed of a lake, an anthill and the doorstep of a prostitute's house.

Naval duties were again interrupted for a visit to Ottawa and a week in Canada's frozen Northwest Territories. In Ottawa he danced with the headline-making Margaret Trudeau, wife of Canada's Prime Minister. Dubbing him 'Crown Prince of Comedy', Canadian papers praised his 'high-voltage charm, quick wit and bubbling fun', adding that he had 'broken down protocol where it has never been broken before'.

There was certainly little enough protocol about his trip to the frozen north, where he descended a goldmine at Yellowknife, lunched with bush pilots, drove a snowmobile, sampled raw seal liver, was shown how to construct an igloo in case he should ever need one in a hurry, tried his hand at handling a team of huskies and made his celebrated dive under the Arctic ice.

The dive, which he made in the company of research scientist Dr John MacInnis, took place at Resolute Bay, some 600 miles inside the Arctic Circle. Wearing two sets of underwear, a rubber suit filled with warm air, six lead weights and two breathing tanks, Charles lowered himself through six feet of ice to dive to a depth variously reported as being thirty feet and fifty feet. Certainly he stayed down for half an hour in water which was 3½ degrees below freezing. It was 'bloody cold', he said later.

Clowning as he so often does, he emerged at the end of his dive from the tent covering the hole in the ice wearing the bowler hat which MacInnis had earlier concealed on the sea-bed and he had retrieved. To everyone's amazement and amusement, he proceeded to inflate his protective suit to Michelin-man-like proportions until he looked, he recalls, like 'a great orange walrus'. Carrying the joke still further, he deflated the suit and let his body crumple with it until he looked, briefly, like nothing so much as a punctured balloon.

Certainly no protocol about all that. Indeed, there was so little protocol about the whole tour that, for once, the barriers which usually separate Britain's royalty from the accompanying pressmen seemed hardly to exist at all. 'One of the best royal tours I have ever covered,' one correspondent assured us.

And that night, at dinner, Charles and his aides, equerry and secretary, physician and detective, won a standing ovation from the press boys for their close harmony barbershop rendering of a witty ditty Charles himself had penned about the 'hazards' of a royal tour.*

Unlike his father, who for all too long seemed to be engaged in a running battle with the press, Charles seems to welcome their attentions. Well, up to a point. Despite his 'terrible' experiences in boyhood when they hounded him so relentlessly, he appreciates that in a day and age when even Royalty must watch its step in Britain if it does not want to go the same way as several other time-honoured institutions, publicity is as important to the Prince of Wales as to any pop singer or movie star. Perhaps more so. 'It's when nobody wants to write about you or take a photograph of you that you ought to worry in my sort of job,' Charles has said.

*APPENDIX VI

328

So he is helpful and co-operative, at least for the most part, with the occasional touch of princely clowning, as in Canada, thrown in for good measure. But he knows that the princely image depends upon more than merely clowning and, in this respect, is his own best public relations man.

When his ship returned to Plymouth in 1974, for instance, he was told that the press would be coming aboard to take pictures. Far from resenting the idea, he came up with a suggestion of his own which he thought would make a very good picture.

'Since I'm flight deck officer,' he said, 'wouldn't it be a good idea if I was seen *doing* one of my jobs which is a new line and a good one to photograph as well?'

The result was the picture of him operating his 'bats' to launch one of the ship's helicopters.

'Compromise,' he says is the essence of his relationship with the press. Only very occasionally does he react after the manner of his sister, though there was a slight—and rare—touch of disgruntlement in the air the day he arrived at HMS

Vernon, the Navy's mine warfare school. Photographers called out for him to look at their cameras.

'I'm not a horse,' he snapped back.

It was a bearded Prince Charles who arrived back in Britain from Blissville Air Force Base, New Brunswick, in late May 1975. But the following day, when he was installed as Great Master of the Most Honourable Order of the Bath in succession to the late Duke of Gloucester, the beard had gone and only a moustache remained. He did not feel that a beard was 'respectable enough' for a public engagement, Charles said.

The newspapers and others were quick to remind him that only a 'full set' was permissible under naval regulations. But Charles had an answer to that. He was also Colonel-in-Chief of the Royal Regiment of Wales, Buckingham Palace reminded the critics. Army officers, of course, are permitted moustaches though not beards.

And it was in his Colonel-in-Chief's uniform, topped with a mantle of crimson satin, that he attended his mother in the Henry VII chapel of Westminster Abbey, promising to defend maidens, widows and orphans, and placing his sword briefly upon the altar as a token of his intention to do so.

But the following day, when he flew out of London again to rejoin the *Hermes* at Halifax, Nova Scotia, moustache as well as beard had gone to comply with naval regulations. 'It feels colder this morning,' he quipped, stroking his clean-shaven chin as he boarded his aircraft.

The summer of 1975 found him riding beside his mother for the first time to the annual Trooping the Colour ceremony on Horse Guards' Parade which traditionally marks the Queen's official (as distinct from her actual) birthday. He wore the uniform of Colonel of the Welsh Guards, a role which, as Prince of Wales, he had now taken over from his father.

The following month, this time in naval uniform, he was at Turnhouse RAF station to welcome King Carl Gustav of Sweden on his four-day state visit to Britain. To mark the occasion, the Queen had given Sweden's young king seniority over her son, appointing him an Admiral of the Fleet, and he changed into the appropriate uniform on the flight over.

In the interval before settling down to his lieutenant's course at the Royal Naval College, Greenwich, Charles flew to Papua New Guinea for yet more independence junketings. Temporarily relinquishing his naval rank to become 'Nambawan pikini blong Misis Kwin,' as he was christened in the local pidgin, he went on from Port Moresby, the capital, to tour the Eastern Highlands, where, among other things, he presented first prize to the winner of a tribal beauty contest, an eighteen-year-old lovely in a feathered head-dress, shell necklace and bark shirt.

Later still that year, over two days salvaged from naval lectures at Greenwich, in his role as president of the Canterbury Cathedral Appeal Fund, he again turned commentator for a television documentary about the cathedral, interviewing the Archbishop, Dr Donald Coggan, as well as the man in charge of repairing the crumbling stonework. The programme was spiced with the usual princely jokes. One of the Black Prince's gilt and copper gauntlets, for instance, became 'a medieval form of knuckleduster'. But his sincere love for the ancient cathedral also showed through in a script which he had partly devised himself. 'Each time (I come here) I am filled with wonder at the sheer feat of engineering that was required to create this sculptured masterpiece. The cathedral has been part of the life and heritage of this country for so many centuries that one almost feels it is something exquisitely fashioned by nature alone rather than man.'

If Charles had indeed 'broken down' protocol during his visit to Ottawa earlier in the year, he was more concerned to uphold it at the silver jubilee dinner of the Lord's Taverners which he attended in November 1975. Together with some 1350 other guests, he had just finished his main course and was about to be served with a sweet in the form of hot cherries and cream when he was asked to propose the Loyal Toast.

'No,' said the Prince firmly, to the amazement of one and all.

Of course, he may not have said it quite so bluntly as that. In the momentary embarrassment which followed no one, afterwards, was quite sure exactly what had been said. But the dialogue between Charles and toastmaster Bryn Williams would seem to have gone something like this:

Charles (as the microphone is plonked in front of him): Do we have to do this now?

Toastmaster: We do, sir.

Charles: Why do we have the Loyal Toast so early? Is this a modern trend?

Toastmaster: I am afraid so, sir.

For the benefit of any Americans who may chance to read this book, we should perhaps interrupt this impromptu crosstalk act to explain that in Britain, at public dinners and the like, it is considered *lèse-majesté* to light up a cigarette before the Loyal Toast—'The Queen'— has been proposed and drunk. Because of this, bodies like the Variety Club of Great Britain, who have a lot of visiting Americans at their charity functions (and Americans, as everyone knows, have an unfortunate habit of smoking almost

334

right through a meal), have developed a tendency to propose the Loyal Toast immediately after the first course. The Lord's Taverners did not go quite as far as that—they waited until after the main course—but it was still too far for Charles.

'Well, I don't agree with it', he told toastmaster Williams. 'I don't like the trend because I don't smoke. We will have the Loyal Toast at the right time—after the sweet.'

And so they did, with those dying for a smoke hastily stuffing their cigarettes back into pockets and handbags.

Of all the Royals—excluding the Queen, who would hardly be found proposing a toast to herself—perhaps only Charles could have got away with it. Had either Philip or Anne been involved, the incident would almost certainly have started a *brouhaha* which would have echoed for days, perhaps weeks, afterwards. But Prince Charles' stand on behalf of protocol, though fully reported in the newspapers, aroused little comment and hardly any adverse criticism, possibly because hardly anyone was quite sure of what was socially correct.

In December, 1976, with his mother's silver jubilee due to be celebrated the following year, Charles said goodbye to the Navy. He had been at sea a little over five years and naval service had never been intended to be more than part of the princely training programme. His departure was in true naval tradition. A lavatory seat bearing the ship's crest was slung round his neck with toilet roll dangling beneath and he was pushed the two hundred yards from ship to car in a squeaky wheelchair adorned with a banner announcing: Command Has Aged Me. The ship's medical assistant gave him a few words of parting advice: 'Keep your bowels open, sir.' More seriously, he added, 'He's been the best skipper in the business.' Mrs Patricia Brotherton would have agreed with that. HMS *Bronington* was at sea with her husband aboard when she gave birth to their baby. Charles not only allowed her husband home the moment they were back in port again, but sent Patricia a telegram: 'My best wishes and congratulations on the birth of your daughter. I apologize for detaining your husband. Charles.'

Charles' main contribution to his mother's silver jubilee was what eventually became the Royal Jubilee Trusts, a fund designed to help youth and community projects. As always, he made full use of television to launch the appeal, raising nearly £16 million from trusts, foundations, industrial concerns and individual donations.

Departure from the Royal Navy was to involve no let-up in travel, however. Indeed, there was more of it than ever: a tour of West Africa; a visit to Canada where the Blackfoot and Blood tribes installed him as Chief Red Crow; a tour of the United States and a visit to Australia. All this in jubilee year. His American tour alone involved touchdowns at Chicago, Atlanta, Charleston, Houston (where he tested his flying skills in a space shuttle simulator), Los Angeles (where he sat between Angie Dickinson and Farah Fawcett-Majors at a charity dinner) and San Francisco.

The following year it was Brazil and Venezuela. Everywhere he went there were pretty girls eager to kiss him, something that would have been unthinkable with a royal prince of any previous generation. 'I just relax and enjoy it,' said Charles, grinning.

He represented his mother at the funeral of the Kenyan president, Jomo Kenyatta; visited Yugoslavia to meet the ageing President Tito; and dropped in on Brussels to look at the headquarters of the European Economic Community.

Another year, other countries. Australia again with a side-trip to Singapore. That was in 1979, a year also marked by personal tragedy.

Charles was not born when his paternal grandfather died in Monte Carlo and has only blurred memories of his maternal grandfather, King George VI, who died when Charles was three. His great-uncle, Earl Mountbatten of Burma, had taken the place of both. They were close to each other, the youthful Prince and the ageing Mountbatten, and each enjoyed the other's company. They were making plans for another visit to India together when Mountbatten met his death, brutally killed when his fishing boat was blown up off the Irish coast by an IRA bomb.

Charles felt the loss of 'Uncle Dickie' keenly and deeply. Grief-stricken and bitter, he shed tears at the memorial service, delivering a eulogy in which he denounced his great-uncle's death as 'mindless cruelty' and labelled the men responsible as 'sub-human'. It was perhaps more than mere coincidence that he paid a flying visit to Northern Ireland a few months later and spent six hours visiting some of the worst trouble spots in South Armagh.

More and more he was proving himself a young man of many talents. Like his father before him, he put a selection of his paintings—water-colours done around Sandringham—on public view. A children's book he had written originally to amuse his younger brothers found a ready publisher and was soon selling like hot cakes. Public speeches were tending to become more outspoken. He became the first-ever Royal to address a trade union conference, telling delegates to the Iron and Steel Trades Confederation: 'We can knock the stuffing out of our competitors from here to Christmas, but we need to understand each other better on both sides of industry. Somehow we seem to lack motivation and inspiration.'

His list of appointments, presidencies and patronages grew quickly now that he was home from the sea, though it will be some time before he can rival his father's staggering collection, if only because he prefers to be associated only with organizations which will let him play an active part—his presidency of the Mary Rose Trust, for instance. In 1979 and 1980 he was again donning diving gear and going down to see how the work of salvaging Henry VIII's famous flagship was coming along. And in accepting the Colonelcy-in-Chief of the Parachute Regiment, he insisted on going along to No 1 Parachute Training School and taking a refresher course.

In 1980 he flew out to Africa again, this time to see Rhodesia become Zimbabwe. Later that year he undertook the tour of India on which Earl Mountbatten had intended to accompany him. The two of them had planned to follow the official part of the tour with a private trek through the foothills of Everest. In the event, Charles made the trek alone. Well, not quite alone, perhaps. The Press made much of the fact that he had some 134 people along with him—ninety porters, twenty-one Sherpas, a support party of eleven, a further eleven royal aides and the King of Nepal's brother. 'Absolutely wonderful; great fun', said Charles when it was all over.

That spell in Nepal had also afforded him a breathing-space, a chance to think...about himself, about his future, about Diana Spencer. With his return to Britain it was only a matter of weeks before he proposed to her.

Their betrothal was hardly more than twenty-four hours old when royal duty parted them, if only briefly. While the bride-to-be collected her personal belongings from her flat and returned to Clarence House to live with the Queen Mother, Charles was on his way to Scotland. Cries of 'Where's the lassie?' greeted him at Greenock and he took the opportunity to get a bit of his own back on the newspaper which had run the

Royal Love Train story. There was something of a problem about being together on the same train, he said, whimsically.

It was during this Scottish trip that Peter Balfour, chairman of the Scottish Council, made a slip of the tongue he will not easily forget. He proposed a lunchtime toast to 'Prince Charles and Lady *Jane*'. Charles blushed beetroot red and the unfortunate Balfour wished the floor would open up and swallow him. 'I feel bloody awful...a perfect fool,' he said afterwards.

The following week saw the Prince and his bride-to-be making their first public appearance together, attending a recital of music, prose and poetry organized to raise money for the Royal Opera House Development Appeal. If only a few hundred people saw the bride-to-be in person that night, millions more gaped delightedly at their screens as the television camera gave them a close-up of her strapless evening gown in black silk taffeta. She was holding a single pink rose which had been thrust into her hand on the steps of Goldsmith's Hall with a card attached: 'To a lovely lady—an

English rose.'

There was a similar romantic touch to her second public engagement, when she accompanied her husband-to-be on a visit to Cheltenham. The couple were waiting to board their helicopter again for the return trip to London when an eighteen-year-old schoolboy, Nicholas Hardy, handed Diana a single daffodil, accompanying the gift with a request: 'May I kiss the hand of my future Queen?'

Opinions differ as to her reply. Was it a straightforward 'Yes, you may', as one newspaper reported, or a more diffident, 'Well, I don't know', as another newspaper reporter thought? Whatever it was, young Nicholas did his kissing act to the delight, and possible envy, of a number of school chums who were with him. 'You will never live this down,' his future Queen told him, with a blushing smile.

That was also the day the marriage was given formal approval as required, because Charles is a descendant of George II, by the Royal Marriage Act of 1772. Prime minister Margaret Thatcher and three former prime ministers were among the twenty-eight members of the Privy Council who were present to hear the Queen utter the one word, 'Consent'. Afterwards a smiling royal mum posed for the first photographs to be taken with her son and future daughter-in-law.

With each fresh public appearance the bride-to-be won her way more deeply into the hearts of the British people... and never more so that the day she journeyed to London airport to see Prince Charles off on a five-week tour of New Zealand, Australia, Venezuela and the United States. They kissed at the foot of the aircraft steps. 'Take care,' he said. Television cameras witnessing the scene showed clearly the tears which started in Diana's eyes at this moment of parting and the struggle she had to keep from openly weeping as her husband-to-be took off.

Charles' last bachelor tour did not get off to a particularly good start. Hardly had he set foot in New Zealand than he was accosted by a bunch of pretty girls all hair-styled, made-up and dressed to look like Lady Diana. Charles can see the amusing side of most situations—as he showed later when he was presented with a matrimonial ball and chain in Auckland; 'I hope it's the right size,' he quipped—but he was no more amused by the Lady Di look-alikes than Queen Victoria would have been, rightly suspecting that it was a photographic ploy. Perhaps, too, there was more than a grain of truth to his later confession at a farewell dinner in Rotorua that he missed Diana and was 'pining' for her.

It was as well perhaps that he did not see another Lady Di look-alike in Australia, a hairdresser named Belinda Lee who had been signed up to promote a brand of mineral water on local televison. But if he did not meet Belinda, there was another young lady down under who came a shade too close for princely comfort the day he went swimming at Bondi beach. Suddenly, almost out of nowhere—another photographic ploy—up popped Bree Summers, a twenty-two-year-old model in bikini pants and a see-through top.

His bodyguard, Chief Inspector John Maclean, called a warning and Charles sprinted hurriedly for his car with Bree in close pursuit until Maclean caught her by the arm. 'That's far enough, miss.'

Less light-heartedly was the situation at Monash University, Melbourne, where a group of students hurled abuse at him. Taken aback, Charles turned ashen. Elsewhere, however, there was a warm welcome from Australians who have rather tended to regard him as their private piece of royal property since his spell at Timbertop. Indeed, there was some talk as to the possibility of him becoming Governor-General in the future.

Like any other young man separated from the girl he loves, Charles telephoned Diana frequently during the course of his tour. Some of these calls were said not only to have been tapped, but taped and hardly was he home again than transcripts of the tapes were being peddled around newspaper offices. Charles and Diana moved quickly to quash the whole business, obtaining injunctions in both Britain and Germany to prohibit publication. Despite this, a German magazine, *Die Acktuelle,* did publish, as did two Irish papers, *Irish Independent* and *Sunday World*, and the rather obscure Australian *Sunday Observer*. Shown transcripts of the tapes, Charles and Diana labelled them as fakes. In the Dorset village of Bere Regis, home of Simon Regan, the freelance journalist responsible for hawking the story, local folk meted out their own form of justice. Regan's car window was smashed and its tyres punctured, while the village store banned him from the premises.

From Australia Charles flew to Venezuela and the United States, where students of the William and Mary university in Williamsburg gave him a rather better reception than he had been accorded at Monash. In his speech there he recalled that Mary had had the misfortune to marry a man (William) who was twelve years her senior. After a pause for the inevitable outburst of laughter, he added, 'I see you are well informed', a joking reference to the similar age gap between himself and his bride-to-be.

In Washington he called on President

Reagan, still recovering from the attempt on his life. It was no more than natural that the steeplechasing prince and the one-time cowboy movie actor should talk horses. 'If you ride horses, you're sometimes going to fall off,' said Charles. The President nodded in sympathetic agreement. 'It doesn't mean you're a bad horseman,' he threw in for good measure.

With Charles' return home, Lady Diana flew to Scotland to meet him and they retreated together to a lodge on the Balmoral estate for a happy reunion. Riding, Diana quickly discovered, was not the only thing she would have to learn if she was to fit into the lifestyle of the Royal Family. There was salmon fishing, too. Suitably clad against the bad weather, she waded into the River Dee for Charles to initiate her into the art of fly-fishing. However, she was less lucky at getting a fish than landing a prince, though her husband-to-be managed to catch two 12-pounders.

In London two alert postal workers at the West Central sorting office drew attention to a padded envelope addressed to the Prince at Buckingham Palace. It proved to be a letter bomb and disposal experts were called in to defuse it. No terrorist organization claimed responsibility, but it was natural that the IRA should be suspected.

The couple's reunion holiday over, Diana settled quickly to the ordeal of the royal round. Shy though she is, her sense of humour won through on more than one public occasion. Their first joint engagement following Charles' return was to open an exhibition at Broadlands, the Mountbatten family home in Hampshire. 'You really are gorgeous,' a man in the crowd told her. 'Don't let my better half hear that,' she riposted laughingly.

Shops, hotels and manufacturers began girding themselves for the expected royal wedding bonanza. The Queen's own shop at Sandringham was quickly in on the act with souvenirs which ranged from locally-made pencils at tenpence each to glass goblets at £35 apiece. Not all souvenirs offered for sale elsewhere were in such good taste. Some, indeed, were downright trashy. If the Lord Chamberlain could do nothing about the flood of cheap foreign imports, he tried to preserve a modicum of good taste where Britain's own products were concerned. Among other things, he pronounced himself as opposed to pictures of Charles and Diana appearing on T-shirts, though he had no objection, he said, to them being seen on tea towels. Some people thought this a load of nonsense and seventy Members of Parliament tabled their opposition to it. The Design Council, too, tried to maintain standards, selecting only sixty out of a thousand souvenirs submitted to it for exhibition. Altogether, by the time the wedding day arrived, an estimated 1,600 different souvenirs were on offer, from boxes of matches at threepence to silver busts at £2,500, from plastic wall plaques to crystal goblets, from beer mats and ashtrays to scarves, medallions and jewellery.

A spate of hardy royal annuals served as a training ground for Lady Diana's future role as Princess of Wales. She went to Royal Ascot, to Wimbledon (where she witnessed some of the tantrums of John McEnroe), joined her future royal in-laws at palace garden-parties and appeared with them on the palace balcony following the Trooping the Colour ceremony.

Her presence made Royal Ascot more like its *My Fair Lady* stage version than ever, with ecstatic cries of 'Aint she bloomin' luverly' (or the equivalent) being heard as she stole the show day after day in a series of eye-catching titfers (tit-for-tats being hats to those unfamiliar with Cockney rhyming slang)... a lilac straw trimmed with osprey, red worn with a candy-striped blouse, peach worn at a fetchingly saucy tilt and an Edwardian-style white straw complete with misty veil and appropriate love-knots.

With her photograph gracing the newspapers nearly every day, you would have thought that there was no one in Britain who would not have recognized her instantly. Not so. Ladies' Day at Ascot found her halted as she was about to enter the Royal Enclosure. 'May I see your badge, please?' gateman Robin Russell requested.

It was not exactly a case of not recognizing her, a red-faced Robin explained later, more a case of 'not looking at faces. You're just looking for badges.'

It was only when someone said, 'That's Lady Diana' that he glanced up and saw who it was. As for Diana, she looked a bit startled at first, but then 'gave me a lovely smile and walked on'.

Prince Charles, who is hardly more enthusiastic about watching horse racing than his father is, gave Ascot a miss on a couple of days in order to fly to New York on a charity fund-raising expedition. As things turned out, he would have been better advised to have remained at home. The trip proved to be a near-fiasco, with Irish-American supporters of the IRA besieging the theatre where the Royal Ballet was giving a gala performance of *The Sleeping Beauty*, banging dustbin lids, shouting abuse and pelting ballet-goers with eggs. A few even penetrated the theatre itself, bringing the show temporarily to a halt with shouts of 'British murderers' and 'prince of killers'. Further insult was added to verbal injury when New York's mayor Ed Koch blabbed to the Press a number of remarks Charles had made to him in private concerning the brutal murder of Earl Mountbatten and the incident at the previous week's Trooping the Colour when a fusillade of blank cartridges had startled the Queen's horse.

In addition to attending so many public functions, Diana somehow found time to sit for the first of what will surely be a production line of portraits. The first one, painted and exhibited while she was still unwed and not yet Princess of Wales, was commissioned by the National Portrait Gallery as a companion piece to one of Prince Charles painted earlier. The same artist, Bryan Organ, painted both. He depicted the future Princess in a trendy outfit of trousers and waistcoat, sitting sideways on a chair, legs crossed, which is about as far removed from the traditional tiara-and-crinoline royal portrait as you could hope to get.

Diana herself and her royal fiancé were both said to be 'delighted' with the result. The National Portrait Gallery certainly was. Its director, Dr John Hayes, waxed almost lyrical in describing the portrait as conveying all the bride-to-be's 'natural warmth, inner strength, outgoing qualities and warmhearted-ness'. Many people, art experts and non-experts alike, were equally lavish in their praise, but not everyone liked the painting.

Charles continued to maintain and embellish his 'Action Man' image. So much so that the wonder was that he finally made it to the altar without an arm in a sling or a foot in plaster. He again went deep-water diving to see how the work of raising Henry VIII's old flagship *Mary Rose* was coming along, he took part in a charity show-jumping event (contriving to stay in the saddle this time) and, only the weekend before the wedding, was twice in action on the polo field. Fortunately, it was not Charles but one of his team-mates who had to quit the field temporarily during one polo game with a bloodied face.

Diana, by then, had celebrated her twentieth birthday. She was still only nineteen when she and Charles visited their future not-terribly-stately home, Highgrove, close to the village of Tetbury in Gloucestershire, to give a garden-party of their own for some five hundred guests, mainly employees of the Duchy of Cornwall and their wives. She was twenty the following day, 1 July, and her future royal in-laws gave a small family party in her honour at Buckingham Palace.

She was still very young, of course; still, despite her crash course in public life, relatively inexperienced. Youth and inexperience, plus perhaps a touch of pre-marriage nerves, found her fleeing in tears from the first of the polo games in which Charles took part the weekend before their wedding. 'Just a temporary upset', a palace spokesman said on her behalf. Charles, as outspoken as ever when it came to dealing with the news-papers and television, was more forth-coming.

'Constantly one hears that she doesn't like watching polo,' he said. 'Absolute rubbish. It isn't much fun when you are surrounded by people with long lenses, poking them from all directions at you almost the entire time, and then taking photos, which it is quite easy to do, and saying "Looking bored". I think all this builds up to a certain amount of strain. And it told eventually. Hardly surprising. I would hope that after we get married it would be easier to come to a polo match without this intensity of interest.'

In hoping that, one fears, he is sighing for the moon. Photographic and journalistic interest in the young lady who is now Princess of Wales is unlikely to diminish for years to come. Given certain circumstances, it could even intensify.

Diana's distress on that occasion was happily short-lived. A good night's rest enabled her again to face the crowds—and the cameras—at Windsor the following day when she watched Charles score one of the goals in England's 10-5 victory over Spain.

To ensure there was no hitch on the actual day, there were a number of rehearsals in advance of the actual wedding. With the bride-to-be looking on, the Lord Chamberlain, Lord Maclean, put the bridesmaids and pages through their paces in St Paul's Cathedral. 'It was basically a reconnaisance for the children to walk the course,' explained a spokesman, rather mixing his military and show-jumping metaphors. Wearing a piece of lace curtain as a wedding veil, Diana herself took part in a subsequent rehearsal, slipping into the cathedral by way of an underground car park to avoid the estimated crowd of 3,000 people massed outside. However, the crowd got what it was waiting for in due course. The rehearsal over, she and Charles came out and down the steps together, hand in hand.

Among the public, wedding fever was building up fast. A processional rehearsal found the route from the palace to the cathedral and the area around the cathedral jam-packed with cars, coaches and people who waved at and cheered the Glass Coach and other carriages for all that they were empty or occupied at most by men from the Lord Chamberlain's office equipped with stop-watches and pocket calculators.

Charles took his own precautions to ensure that there was no wedding day hitch on his part, no hint such as was made about his father's wedding day that he might be suffering from a slight hang-over. His farewell bachelor party was held not the night before the wedding, as Prince Philip's had been, but a full week earlier. Nor, by all accounts, was it any-where near as boisterous as father's had been, but a fairly quiet, rather sedate affair at White's, London's oldest pri-vate club, of which he is a member, with fewer than twenty guests sitting down to a cold collation accompanied by appropriate wines.

As day after day was crossed off towards the red-letter date on Diana's calendar, everyone who conceivably could seemed determined to get in on the act, and not only souvenir manufac-turers. Wine sales soured as *vin ordinaire* appeared in bottles with such elegant and appropriate labels as 'Royal Marriage'. Entrepreneurs were busy buying up the most advantageous window space over-looking the processional route (and some of them were to catch a slight financial cold in consequence). The Royal Mint issued a special silver crown and the Post Office came up with special stamps. Madame Tussauds refurbished its waxwork model of Prince Charles and installed a new one of his bride-to-be. British Rail named one of its engines *Lady Diana Spencer.* The wonder was that British Gas did not do the same with one of its cookers.

Advice for future marital happiness was forthcoming on all sides. The Archbishop of Canterbury, Dr Robert Runcie, took the opportunity of a consultative meeting with the couple to deliver a few homelies on the subject of marriage, sex and parenthood. Sex, he told them, was 'a good thing, given by God, which nevertheless, like all God's gifts, needs to be directed aright'. The magazine *Family,* a copy of which was despatched *gratis* to the happy pair was a shade more forthcoming. 'Seek to satisfy your partner's needs. Take time to make love.'

The Poet Laureate, Sir John Betjeman, although a sick man, penned a poem in honour of the occasion, comments on which ranged from 'charming' to 'uninspired'. Comedian Spike Milligan managed to get in slightly ahead of him with a rather longer effusion in the style of Willie McGonagall, the Scottish poetaster of Victorian times. Space permits the quotation of only a fragment.

Lady Di sent off a list of presents
they'd like,
Some fish forks, a toaster and a bike,
A cookbook, some plates, a potted
dahlia,
And the head of a telephone engineer
in Australia.

The reference to the telephone engineer, of course, harked back to the earlier rumpus when someone was said to have taped Charles' private telephone calls to his fiancée while touring Australia. The other fifty-odd lines of Milligan's verse were in similar irreverent vein. Even in Henry VIII's day, a court jester could always get away with more than most and Milligan proved no exception. Instead of cries of 'Off with his head', he was invited to the wedding. So was fellow former Goon, Harry Secombe.

The complete guest list yielded a pretty mixed bag, comics as well as kings, pop stars as well as princes. Some of the bridegroom's former girl friends were invited along with the bride's former flatmates, Virginia Pitman, Carolyn Pride and Anne Bolton. The bridegroom also invited people he had known in schooldays, at university and in the Navy, including Peter Beck, the headmaster who caned the princely bottom during his time at Cheam. The bride invited Nina Missetsiz, the diminutive Greek seamstress who cut and stitched her wedding dress, along with the young people who designed it and her hairdresser. These were only a few of many, of course, and even with seating space for some 2,600 guests at the wedding, the invitation list proved something of a problem. There was a whole shoal of relatives on both sides to be invited, of course; royal staff from Windsor, Sandringham, Balmoral; monarchs from Europe and elsewhere; heads of Commonwealth countries; and, because the wedding was also a state occasion however much the bridegroom's mother might prefer to look upon it as 'a family affair', presidents, politicians, ambassadors and other such notables. 'It has been quite difficult on my side,' Diana revealed once the invitations had gone out. 'To have a certain amount, you have to sort of take people out.'

Taking people out meant that some who had hoped to be invited were disappointed. Equally, however, some who were invited chose to decline their invitations, among them Ken Livingstone, left-wing head of the Greater London Council, who preferred to spend a day working and then go on to a rock concert.

A more important absentee was King Juan Carlos of Spain. Having originally accepted an invitation to the wedding, he felt unable to attend, for all that he was a distant relative, after it had been announced that bride and groom, as part of their honeymoon, would be flying to Gibraltar to board the royal yacht *Britannia* for a Mediterranean cruise. The ownership of Gibraltar has been a touchy question between Britain and Spain for years and, for all the criticism levelled at Juan Carlos in the House of Commons, there were many who sympathized with him in his personal-political dilemma.

Good luck telegrams, letters, gifts from all parts of the world were received in such numbers that the palace post office was in grave danger of disappearing under the deluge. By the weekend before the wedding more than 3,000 gifts and a staggering 100,000 letters had been opened and listed for acknowledgement and thanks, with a further forty sacks of packages and mail stacked in the palace corridors awaiting attention. Few brides get *everything* they have detailed on their gift list. Lady Diana did. Inevitably, as with most brides, there was some duplications. Not that it mattered. 'We've two homes to furnish,' the bride-to-be pointed out. One was Highgrove, the Gloucestershire mansion not far from the princess—Anne—who would soon be her sister-in-law. Anne's nearby country home, Gatcombe Park, had been bought for her by her mother. Charles' and Diana's future home was bought by Charles himself out of the Duchy of Cornwall monies. The second home to which Diana referred was the Kensington Palace apartment which would serve as their London base.

By the eve of the wedding the processional route between the palace and St Paul's was thick with deck-chairs, sleeping-bags, air-beds, car seats and even armchairs as thousands of people, determined to get a front-row view, camped out on the pavements. For a few of the hardier loyalists it was their third night of sleeping rough. Curiously, interviewed as to what they were doing there, few said they had come to see the wedding procession. They had come to see Lady Di, they said, further evidence of the way the nation had taken this shyly attractive girl to its heart. Union Jacks were in evidence everywhere. They fluttered not only from buildings, but were to be seen on hats, socks, T-shirts and, as one young lady daringly revealed, even took the form of bikini bras. Not to be outdone, one young man wandered around with his face transformed into a Union Jack by the application of red, white and blue make-up. The whole of the processional route was fast turning into one vast street party with people bathing in the fountain at Trafalgar Square and dancing in the approach road to St Paul's. Most were native Brits, of course, but there was also a substantial leavening of people from Australia, Canada, New Zealand, America and elsewhere.

Diana had been staying temporarily at Buckingham Palace. On the wedding eve, after an afternoon in the country with Charles, she left there to return again to Clarence House where the two grandmothers, the Queen Mother and Ruth, Lady Fermoy, could give her those bits of womanly advice grandmothers invariably give to young brides. Charles spent the evening with his parents and a whole host of top brass wedding guests watching a fireworks display in Hyde Park. Diana preferred an early night to bolster her against the nervous strain of the wedding day. In any event, tradition demands that the bride does not permit her future husband to see her on their wedding eve.

An estimated half a million people crowded into Hyde Park for the fireworks display, the biggest of its kind to be staged in Britain for more than two hundred years. Complete with military bands, massed choirs and the guns of the King's Troop of Royal Horse Artillery, it was in fact a repeat performance of the fireworks and musical extravaganza of 1749 for which Handel composed the original music. Charles himself, in the centre of the vast, open-air arena, set off a flare which was the signal for a chain of 101 celebration bonfires to blaze from hill tops and similar vantage points throughout the length and breadth of Britain. No need for Ken Livingstone and other left-wingers to moan at the cost, for the sale of television rights not only recouped all expenses but also made a profit for charity.

After weeks of almost unremitting wind and rain, Britain's always uncertain weather had turned fair. The wedding day itself dawned bright and sunny, so perpetuating the myth of 'Queen's weather'—that the Queen shall have sunshine wherever she goes (which certainly was not the case on the day of her coronation). 'I can't believe the weather,' the Queen said delightedly as she gazed out of the palace windows.

To longtime observers of the royal

scene, like ourselves, the wedding of Charles, Prince of Wales, to the Lady Diana Spencer on 29 July, 1981 showed yet again that things go in cycles. When the bridegroom's parents were married in the postwar era of 1947, a time of shortages and rationing, Winston Churchill, with his gift for finding the right phrase, spoke of it as 'a joyous event...a flash of colour on the hard road we have to travel'. Nearly thirty-four years later the marriage of their eldest son was to provide another 'flash of colour' on a road made no less hard by the evils of inflation, unemployment, riots, left-wing agitation and international terrorism... another 'joyous event' which drew people to London in their tens of thousands from all parts of Britain, from the far corners of the Commonwealth and what little still remained of the old British Empire, from countries as far apart as America and Japan.

'No feeling would seem more childish than the enthusiasm of the English at the marriage of the Prince of Wales... They treated it as a great political event. But no feeling could be more like human nature as it is or as it is likely to be. Women care fifty times more for a marriage than a ministry.' So wrote Walter Bagehot, the eminent Victorian historian. The marriage he referred to was that of the Prince of Wales who later became King Edward VII. His words were perhaps even more applicable 118 years later to the wedding of today's infinitely more popular Prince of Wales.

If the Queen preferred to look upon the occasion as 'a family affair', it was equally a television spectacular, with cameramen and commentators descending on London from all parts of the world. Their joint outpourings were seen and heard by an estimated world-wide audience of some 750 million people in fifty-five countries, some of whom, in places as far ahead of Greenwich time as Australia or as far behind as California, stayed up far into the night or even all through the night until they were bleary-eyed with watching, 'squared-eyed', as Charles himself put it. Even Spain, despite its disagreement with Britain over the inclusion of Gibraltar in the honeymoon itinerary, had three and a half hours of live television coverage while South Africa showed everything that was not banned by those choristers and musicians taking part in the wedding service who were members of Equity or the Musicians' Union.

It was, also, as much a state occasion as a family affair, with a guest list which included King Olaf of Norway, King Carl Gustav and Queen Silvie of Sweden, the King and Queen of the Belgians, Queen Margrethe and Prince Henry of Denmark, Queen Beatrix and Prince Claus of the Netherlands, Princess Grace of Monaco, the Crown Princes of Jordan and Japan, the 350-pound King of Tonga (who brought his own outsize chair to St Paul's with him), other kings and ex-kings, queens and ex-queens, princes and princesses, grand dukes, America's first lady, Nancy Reagan, the Governor-General of Australia, the prime ministers of Canada and New Zealand and the presidents of Germany, Portugal, France, India, Zambia and elsewhere.

The Archbishop of Canterbury was sensible enough not to compare it, as a predecessor compared the wedding of the then Princess Elizabeth, nearly thirty-four years before, to that of 'any cottager who might be married in some small village church'. With an escort of Household Cavalry for the bridegroom, the bride arriving in a fairy-tale Glass Coach, with state trumpeters, massed choirs, orchestras and a soprano imported all the way from New Zealand, it could hardly be that. But it was certainly, as the Archbishop chose to put it, 'the stuff of which fairy tales are made'.

In the aftermath of the assassination attempts on President Reagan and the Pope, to say nothing of the discharge of blanks at the Trooping the Colour, there was inevitably a more down-to-earth side to the occasion also. If the soldiers, sailors and airmen lining the two-mile route between palace and cathedral still faced ceremonially inwards, the policemen behind them did not. They faced the crowds, eyes flickering for any sign of possible disturbance. Armed plain-clothes men moved among the crowds and police marksmen with fieldglasses and snipers' rifles kept watch from rooftops and upper windows. Sniffer dogs and metal detectors were employed in the hunt for possible explosives; even sewers passing under the processional route were checked. More armed detectives, wearing footmen's liveries borrowed from the palace, rode on the back of the landaus which conveyed monarch and heir to the wedding ceremony.

There were those among the royal advisers who would have preferred both to have travelled in closed cars. The Queen would not have it. 'Danger,' she said once, 'is part of the job'. So while visiting Royals from Norway, Sweden, Denmark, Belgium, the Netherlands and elsewhere were whipped to the cathedral in a cavalcade of Rolls Royces, the Queen and others of the family trotted there and back in a procession of open landaus. Doubtless the accompanying escort of Household Cavalry had carefully re-rehearsed the manoeuvre first worked out when the Queen visited York some years earlier in defiance of an assassination threat, whereby they could close up round the landaus at the first hint of danger, thus shielding the Queen and others with their bodies and those of their horses. In the event, the fairy-tale quality of the wedding day was marred by nothing more serious than a few arrests for offences like picking pockets.

Getting bride as well as groom, plus others of the family, to the church on time, was a combined military and police operation with officials from the Lord Chamberlain's office and the staff of the Royal Mews thrown in for good measure. For the Queen's procession there was a Sovereign's Escort of Household Cavalry under the command of Lieutenant-Colonel Andrew Parker-Bowles, a close friend of both Charles and Anne. Earlier in the week he had been one of the godparents when Anne's second child was christened Zara Anne Elizabeth and later on the wedding day he was to command the smaller escort which ensured that the newlyweds went safely off on honeymoon. Nearly every member of the Royal Family with the exception of babes-in-armes like Anne's daughter took part in the procession, from the Queen Mother, eighty-one only a few days later, and Princess Alice of Gloucester, fast approaching eighty, to

the five-year-old Earl of Ulster. A
stumble on steps at Ascot the previous
month had caused an ulcer to develop on
the Queen Mother's leg. As dutiful as
always, her leg in bandages, she still insisted on going ahead with a planned visit
to Canada, carrying out every scheduled
engagement there. As a result, the injury
became infected and there was doubt at
one time whether she would make it to
the wedding. But she was determined to
see her favourite grandson married, and
she did. 'I wouldn't have missed this for
anything', she told others of the family.

For the bridegroom there was a Prince
of Wales' Escort of Household Cavalry.
He was accompanied in the landau
built originally for his great-great-grandfather, Edward VII, by Prince Andrew,
one of the two brotherly "supporters"
entrusted with the task of seeing him
safely married. Both were in naval
uniform, Andrew in his rank of midshipman and Charles more resplendant in the
dress uniform of a Royal Navy commander further embellished with the sash
and insignia of the Order of the Garter,
the insignia of the Order of the Thistle,

the cross of Grand Master of the Order of the Bath and his RAF wings.

They were reinforced at the cathedral by younger brother Edward, elegant in his morning suit. Lofty, too, for his seventeen years, as though eventually he might outstrip father and brothers alike, in height. 'You both ready?' Charles asked. 'Right. Come on then.' He had smiled and waved at the crowds on his way to the cathedral. Now tension took over. He massaged his forehead with his fingers and mopped his face with a handkerchief. Andrew kept checking that he still had the ring, fashioned from the same lump of Welsh gold as the wedding rings of the Queen and Queen Mother. As the bridegroom and his supporters awaited the arrival of the bride, their father tried to ease the tension with a teasing joke. 'I remember *your* wedding,' the Queen Mother interposed with a tell-tale smile.

Both the bridegroom and his mother had been greeted on their arrival at the cathedral with bursts of the National Anthem. For the bride, because she was not yet, for a few minutes more, a member of the Royal Family, there was no such greeting. Nor was there an escort of Household Cavalry but mounted policemen instead.

She had been up since shortly after six o'clock, watching televison while her make-up was applied by Barbara Daly, hair styled by Kevin Shanley and Nina Missetsiz ironed the last few creases out of the wedding dress designed for her by David and Elizabeth Emanuel. Only a handful of people were privileged to glimpse the dress as, escorted by her father, Earl Spencer, she climbed into the Glass Coach, bought originally for the coronation of King George V, in the forecourt of Clarence House. Nor could much be glimpsed of it as she followed the by now well-worn route to the cathedral. Not until she descended from the coach on arrival at St Paul's did the world get its first real look at the dress which had been the subject of so much speculation. Fashion copyists, glued to television sets, were speedily at work and by the time bride and groom sat down to their wedding breakfast a few hours later the first quick copies were already on display in Oxford Street stores.

Of course, with time and cost against them, the copyists could come only approximately close to the original with its pie-crust neckline and balloon sleeves, its boned bodice of antique lace and ivory silk taffeta, its crinoline skirt and enormous twenty-five-feet train, its hand embroidery of pearls and mother-of-pearl sequins. Her veil too, of ivory silk tulle, suspended from the Spencer family diamond tiara, was embroidered with mother-of-pearl and her white and yellow bouquet—yellow Earl Mountbatten roses—dripped from her hand like a miniature waterfall. Something old, something new, something borrowed, something blue...so runs the old superstition governing what brides should wear. The old was the antique lace, which had once belonged to Queen Mary. Dress, veil and the matching silk slippers were new enough. Something borrowed were the diamond ear-rings belonging to her mother. The blue was a small blue bow tucked away in the waistband of the dress. 'You look lovely,' Charles told her. But that was later, after the ceremony was over and nervous tension had eased. For the bride, arriving at the cathedral, there was concern too on account of her father's health. Having discarded the walking-stick he normally used since suffering a brain hae-morrhage, he had to have help to climb the steep flight of cathedral steps.

'Are you all right?' his daughter asked him, anxiously. More gallantly than truthfully perhaps, he assured her that he was. 'But go slowly,' he added.

She took his arm and they started up the aisle followed by the bridesmaids in their Victorian-style, ballerina length dresses, the four youngest with floral coronets on their heads. Princess Mar-garet's daughter, Sarah, was chief brides-maid. The others were India Hicks, granddaughter of the late Earl Mount-batten, Sarah-Jane Gaselee, whose father is the Prince's racing trainer, Catherine Cameron, whose parents are among his close friends and the diminu-tive Clementine Hambro, granddaughter of Lord Soames. The two pageboys were the Duke of Kent's younger son, Nicho-las, and Edward Van Cutsem, whose parents are other friends of Prince Charles. If Diana had a hand in deciding what bride and bridesmaids should wear, Charles could equally claim that it was his idea that the youthful pages should be garbed in replica naval uniforms of 1863.

The cathedral was crammed...with choirs, orchestras, Yeomen of the Guard and Gentlemen at Arms in addition to the 2,600 guests. Perhaps 3,500 people in all. Even so, room was somehow found at the back for the contingent lining the steps outside. 'Let them squeeze in and see the wedding,' Charles said when he heard that they would be standing down briefly between the bride's arrival and the departure of bride and groom some eighty minutes later. It was his idea, too, that disabled people, in the Year of the Disabled for which he had done so much, should be given a special place in the palace forecourt from which to see the Royals depart and return.

He wanted his wedding, he said, to be 'a marvellous musical and emotional experience'. It was one of the reasons he and Diana picked St Paul's instead of Westminster Abbey. 'Musically speaking, it is such a magnificent setting and the whole acoustics are so spectacular.' The result matched, perhaps exceeded expectations, with contributions from the state trumpeters, three orchestras, the Bach Choir (of which Charles is president) as well as the cathedral choir and an aria from *Samson And Delilah* sung by the New Zealand Maori soprano Kiri Te Kanawa. Charles himself picked one of the hymns, 'Christ Is Made The Sure Foundation', and Diana another, 'I Vow To Thee My Country', a favourite of hers since schooldays. There was also a new hymn specially composed for the wedding by Dr William Matthias, Head of Music at the University College of North Wales, 'Let The People Praise Thee, O God'.

The marriage service was performed by the Archbishop of Canterbury in new vestments which almost outdid the bride in splendour. He hoped he didn't look too much like something out of *Star Wars,* he joked to Prime Minister Margaret Thatcher before the ceremony. He was assisted by the Dean of St Paul's, the Very Revd Alan Webster. The lesson was read by George Thomas, Speaker of the House of Commons, in his mellifluous Welsh voice. Prayers were said by the Right Revd Lord Coggan, former Archbishop of Canterbury, Cardinal Basil Hume, Roman Catholic Archbishop of Westminster, the Right Revd Dr Andrew Doig, Moderator of the General Assembly of the Church of Scotland, and the Revd Harry Williams, who was Dean of Trinity in the days when Charles was an undergraduate there, to whom fell the honour of referring to the bride for the first time as 'Diana, Princess of Wales'.

Inevitably, small things went wrong. Thanks to the deftness of the chief bridesmaid, the bride's train, lengthy though it was, did not snag on anything as the Queen's had done at her wedding. But the bride, flustered by nerves, or perhaps excitement, took 'Philip Charles Arthur George' instead of 'Charles Philip Arthur George' as her wedded husband. Doubtless her newly-acquired father-in-law teased her about that later. And the bridegroom promised the bride a share of 'all thy goods' (or so it sounded) instead of 'all my wordly goods'.

But it was no mistake that the new Princess of Wales, like the young Danish-born Duchess of Gloucester before her, promised only to love, honour, comfort and keep her husband, not to obey him. Charles was fully in accord with her wish to update the marriage vow in this fashion. The inclusion of 'obey' was simply 'the relic of a past culture,' he said.

Despite these few small mistakes, the service as a whole was a magnificent—and moving—occasion. Charles, a young man in whom emotion runs close to the surface, had joked earlier that he would probably find the ceremony so moving that he would spend 'half the time in tears'. That was not quite the case, though the singing of the first hymn caused tears to start sufficiently for him to have to brush his eyes. Not that he was alone in falling briefly victim to the emotion of the moment. There were times too in the course of the ceremony when both his mother and grandmother brushed away tears. Equally, however, there was a moment when Charles came close to an attack of the giggles as a flamboyant conducting flourish from the St Paul's choirmaster sent one of the lampshades flying.

A lucky horseshoe, secreted inside the landau by someone in the Royal Mews, faced the newlyweds as they trotted back to the palace while the bells of St Paul's pealed an acclamation which was taken up by the 'oranges and lemons' bells of St Clement Danes and other churches across London. Crowds ten and more deep, an estimated total of anything up to a million people, cheered them every yard of the way before converging on the palace in a solid, loyal enthusiastic mass chanting 'We want Charlie' and 'Di, Di, Di'. Officially, the girl who had been Diana Spencer was now Princess Charles, but in the popular mind she will doubtless always be Diana or the more homely Di. Later there were to be chants of 'We want the Queen' and inevitably, so deep and secure is her place in the heart of the nation, 'We want the Queen Mum'.

The Royals responded to the chants with appearances on the palace balcony, the focal point of national emotion so many times in the past, bride and groom, bridesmaids, supporters and pageboys, parents and grandmothers from both sides. It was Andrew, as much a joker at twenty-one as he was in childhood, but with a distinct flair for doing exactly the right thing at the right moment, who murmured to Charles: 'Give her a kiss.'

Charles was hesitant. 'They're trying to get us to kiss,' he whispered to his new young bride.

For all her shyness, Diana, it seemed, had had the same idea herself. Or maybe Andrew had already had a word with her.

'I tried to ask you,' she said.

'How about it?'

'Why not?'

So they kissed, in full view of everyone, the excited thousands massed in front of the palace and the millions more glued to television screens around the world.

Queen Victoria would not have been amused. Even the Queen's father would not have approved of so public a display of affection. But in this day and age it was exactly the right touch.

Then it was inside the palace, for wedding photographs, for a wedding breakfast of chicken breasts stuffed with lamb mousse, quenelles of brill in lobster sauce, strawberries and cream, claret and champagne, for toasts proposed by Andrew and Edward, and for the cutting of the five-tier cake made by HMS Pembroke (which is the Royal Navy Cookery School). Charles unsheathed his dress sword to make the first cut into the bottom layer.

Andrew had a few more tricks up his sleeve, as the newlyweds discovered when they emerged from the palace to climb into the landau which was to take them to Waterloo station. With Edward's help, he had tied a mass of heart-shaped blue and silver balloons to the rear of the conveyance. But even that was not enough for Andrew's outsize sense of humour. Hurriedly, with red crayon, he scrawled a large 'Just Married' announcement decorated with arrow-pierced hearts which he fixed to the back of the landau.

If the bride's wedding dress, magnificent though it was, was perhaps more in the traditional royal style than some had expected, her coral pink going-away outfit of bolero jacket and side-slit skirt, designed by Belinda and David Sassoon, and her plumed tricorne principal girl's hat by John Boyd, echoed youth and freshness. And starting off as one hopes she will be permitted to go on, the new, young Princess of Wales brought her own touch of informality to the departure scene at Waterloo by planting thank-you kisses on the cheeks of the Lord Chamberlain and his comptroller, Lieutenant-Colonel Johnston, who, as their final duty on wedding day, were there to see them safely aboard the train which was to take them to Broadlands.

And there, at Broadlands, the Mountbatten home where the bridegroom's mother also started her honeymoon nearly thirty-four years earlier—because honeymoons, whether for the Prince and Princess of Wales or any ordinary young couple, are essentially private affairs—we will leave them, newlyweds who will one day, all things being equal, be King and Queen. May their married life be long, happy and fruitful.

APPENDICES

APPENDIX I

Appointments, Presidencies, Patronages
held by Prince Charles

Appointments: Counsellor of State
(1966—), Personal ADC to the Queen
(1973—), Privy Councillor (1977—);
Colonel-in-Chief, Royal Regiment of
Wales (1969), Cheshire Regiment (1977),
Gordon Highlanders (1977), Parachute
Regiment (1977), Lord Strathcona's Horse
(Royal Canadian) Regiment (1977), Royal
Regiment of Canada (1977), Royal Wini-
peg Rifles (1977), Royal Australian Ar-
moured Corps (1977), 2nd King Edward
VII's Own Gurkhas (1977), Air Reserve
Group of Air Command (1977);
Colonel, Welsh Guards (1975); Air
Commodore-in-Chief, Royal New Zea-
land Air Force (1977); Hon. Air Commo-
dore, RAF Brawdy (1977).
Presidencies: Welsh Environment Foun-
dation (1971), Welsh Committee, Euro-

pean Architectural Heritage Year (1972), British Sub-Aqua Club (1974), Lord's Taverners (1975-6), Royal Aero Club (1975-80), Cambridge University Polo Club (1975-9), Prince of Wales' Company Club, Welsh Guards (1975—), Wells Cathedral Appeal Trust (1976—), Commonwealth Youth Exchange Council (1977-81), Queen's Silver Jubilee Trust (1977—), National Rifle Association (1977-82), Printers Charitable Corporation (1977), Royal Bath and West Show (1977), Underwater Conservation Year (1977), Youth and Music (1977-9), Friends of Covent Garden (1978—), Highland Society of London (1978-9), Peterborough Royal Foxhound Show (1978), Exeter Cathedral Preservation Trust (1978—), Royal Agricultural Society of England (1978), United World Colleges (1978-82), Devon County Show (1979), Cornwall Crafts Association (1979-83), Scottish Salmon Angling Federation (1979-83), Underwater Conservation Society (1979-84), Royal Naval Equestrian Association (1979—), Wildfowl Trust (1979-84), Royal Smithfield Club (1980), Royal Naval Film Corporation (1980—); Vice-President, Society of the Friends of St George's and Descendants of Knights of the Garter (1968—); Chairman, Steering Committee Welsh Countryside in 1970 Conference (1968-70), Prince of Wales' Committee for Wales (1970—), Canterbury Cathedral Appeal Fund (1974-9), King George's Jubilee Trust (1974-8), Silver Jubilee Appeal (1977); Hon. Comm., Coastguard Service (1980-5).

Patron: Royal Regiment of Wales Association (1969—), Royal Regiment of Wales Officers' Dining Club (1969—), Wales in Bloom Campaign (1970-5), United Nations Organization 25th Anniversary (1970), Joint Services Expedition to the Elephant Island Group (1970-1), Wiltons Music Hall Trust (1971), Royal Asiatic Society (1972—), Royal Anthropological Society (1972-8), Somerset County Federation of Young Farmers' Clubs (1973-6), Bath Preservation Trust (1973-8), Friends of Brecon Cathedral (1974—), League of Venturers (1974—), Thames Angling Preservation (1974-81), Elgar Foundation (1975-80), Game Fair (1975-80), Royal Opera House (1975-80),

British and Royal Nepalese Army Expedition to Mount Everest (1976), Australian Jubilee Appeal Trust (1977—), Royal Tournament (1977—), Joint Services Sub-Aqua Expedition (1977), British Flight Team (1977-9, extended), English Chamber Orchestra and Music Society (1977-82), Operation Drake (1977-80), Royal Cornwall Yacht Club (1977—), Society for the Promotion of Nature Conservation (1977-82), Society of Friends of Royal Naval Museum, Portsmouth (1977—), Welsh Association of Male Voice Choirs (1977-82), Transglobe Expedition (1977-81), British North Polar Expedition (1977-9), York Archaeological Trust (1977-9), Australian and New Zealand Schools Exploring Society (1978-83), British Deer Society (1978-83), British Surfing Association (1978-82), Council for British Archaeology (1978-83), City Arts Festival (1978), Joint Services Expedition to the Chagos Archipelago (1978), Men of Trees Society (1978), National Ski Federation of Great Britain (1978), Old Cranwellian Association (1978), Abbeyfield Society (1979-

85), Chester Cathedral (1979—), British Cultural Festival Mexico (1979), Devon Cattle Breeders' Society (1979-84), Ironbridge Gorge Museum Development (1979-84), Police Foundation (1979-84), Inland Waterways Association (1979), British Film Institute (1979), Flying Doctor Service, UK Branch (1979), Friends of Exeter Cathedral (1979), Hunt Benefit Society (1979), National Anglers' Council (1979), Princess Louise Scottish Hospital (1979), Royal Naval Benevolent Trust (1979), Welsh Appeal (1979), Welsh Rubgy Union Charitable Trusts (1979), Australian Musical Foundation in London (1980-5), Bristol and Welsh Orthopaedic Trust (1980—), Chindits Old Comrades Association (1980-5), Canadian Underwater Councils (1980-5), HMS *Kelly* Reunion Association (1980-5), Intermediate Technology Development Group (1980-5), National Spinal Injuries Centre (1980-1), International Year of Disabled People (1980-1), Philharmonic Orchestra (1980-5), Welsh Black Cattle Society (1980-5), Orders and Medals Research Society (1980—), Parachute Regimental Association (1980—), Tarporley Hunt Club (1980—), Great Japanese Exhibition (1981-2), Vikings in England Exhibition (1981-2), Canadian Warplane Heritage (1981—), Press Club (1982-3), Vice-Patron, Royal Institution (1979—), Royal National College for the Blind (1979—).

APPENDIX II

Education

1956-7   Two Terms (somewhat inter-rupted by ill health) at Hill House, a private day school in London

1957-62   Cheam preparatory school

1962-5   Gordonstoun

1964   Won the Duke of Edinburgh's Award (bronze)

1965   Won the Duke of Edinburgh's Award (silver)

1966   Two terms at Timbertop, a branch of the Geelong Church of England Grammar School, Melbourne, Australia

1966-7   Back to Gordonstoun. Became head of house and then Guardian (head boy of school)

1967-9   Trinity College, Cambridge

1969   One term at the University College of Wales, Aberystwyth

1969-70   Back to Trinity. Graduated Bachelor of Arts (Cantab.) June 1970

APPENDIX III

Princes of Wales

	Date created
Edward (Edward II)	1301
Edward (Black Prince), son of Edward II	1343
Richard (Richard II), son of Black Prince	1377
Henry of Monmouth (Henry V)	1399
Edward of Westminster, son of Henry VI	1454
Edward (Edward V)	1472
Edward, son of Richard III	1483
Arthur, son of Henry VII	1489
Henry (Henry VIII)	1503
Henry, son of James I	1610
Charles (Charles I)	1616
Charles (Charles II)	1630
James, the Old Pretender	1688
George (George II)	1714

Frederick, son of George II	1727
George (George III)	1751
George (George IV)	1762
Albert Edward (Edward VII)	1841
George (George V)	1901
Edward (Edward VIII, Duke of Windsor)	1910
Charles	1958

APPENDIX IV

Principal Overseas Tours and Visits (other than naval tours of duty, for which see Appendix V)

1966   Three-day visit to Mexico before joining the Duke of Edinburgh in Jamaica for the Commonwealth Games
1967   Represented the Queen at the funeral service for Mr Harold Holt, the Australian prime minister
1969   Visited Malta for the bi-centenary celebrations of the University of Malta and to inaugurate a new university campus at Msida
1970   As chairman of the Countryside in 1970 Committee for Wales, attended the Council of Europe's Conservation Conference at Strasbourg with the Duke of Edinburgh
Joined the Queen, Duke and Princess Anne for a tour of Australia, followed

visit to New Zealand

Visited Japan and saw Expo 70 at Osako

Visited Ottawa for two days before being joined by the Queen, Duke and Princess Anne for a 10-day tour of Canada

With Princess Anne, went on to pay a three-day visit to Washington as guests of the Nixons

Represented the Queen at the independence celebrations in Fiji, followed by a visit to the Gilbert and Ellice Islands

Attended the 350th anniversary of the Bermuda Parliament and afterwards visited Barbados

Represented the Queen at the memorial service for General de Gaulle in Paris

1971   Spent two-week holiday in Kenya with Princess Anne. Visited the 1st Batt., Royal Regiment of Wales at Osnabruck, Germany

1972   Joined the Queen and Duke for part of a state visit to France

Three-day visit to Berlin for military and civil engagements

1973   Visited the Royal Regiment of Wales in Germany

Opened the newly restored Prince of Wales' Bastion at St Kitts

Visited the Bahamas as the Queen's representative at the independence celebrations

1974   Joined the Queen, Duke, Anne and Mark for the Commonwealth Games in New Zealand. Later that year he again flew to New Zealand, this time for the funeral of Mr Norman Kirk, the prime minister

Represented the Queen at the centenary celebrations in Fiji and went on to inaugurate the Anglo-Australian telescope at Siding Spring, Australia. Visited other places, including Tasmania, at the same time

1975   Spent a day in New Delhi on his way to Nepal where he represented the Queen at the coronation of King Birendra

Paid a three-day visit to Ottowa followed by a week in Canada's Northwest Territories

Represented the Queen at the independence celebrations in Papua New Guinea

Visited the Royal Regiment of Wales in Berlin

Private visits to the Bahamas, Iceland, Bali and the Netherlands

1976   Attended the Olympic Games

in Montreal, Canada, and had a fishing holiday in Iceland

1977   Paid official visits to Ghana, the Ivory Coast, Monaco, Canada (where he opened the Calgary Stampede), the United States, Australia and Germany (where he visited the 1st Batt., Welsh Guards)

Went on safari in Kenya, fished in Iceland, skied and played polo in France, and sunned himself in the Bahamas

1978   Paid official visits to Brazil, Venezuela, Yugoslavia, Belgium (where he visited EEC, NATO and SHAPE headquarters) and went three times to Germany to visit the Cheshire Regiment and the Parachute Regiments

Went to Australia for the funeral of Sir Robert Menzies, to Kenya for the funeral of Jomo Kenyatta and to Norway for the 75th birthday of King Olaf

Fished in Iceland, played polo in France and holidayed in Spain as guest of the Duke of Wellington

1979   Paid official visits to Hong Kong, Singapore, Australia, Canada, Germany (where he visited the Parachute Regiment) and France. Skied in Switzerland, fished in Iceland and relaxed in the Bahamas

1980   Attended independence celebrations in Zimbabwe

Paid official visits also to Canada, France, India and Nepal

Went to the Netherlands for the accession of Queen Beatrix

Skied in Switzerland, played polo in the United States, fished in Iceland and holidayed in the Bahamas

1981   With his wedding only four months away, Charles was obliged to leave Lady Diana behind while on a five-week tour of New Zealand, Australia, Venezuela and the United States

APPENDIX V

Flying and Naval Career

14 Jan. 1969   First solo flight
March 1970   Obtained Grade A (private pilot) Licence
March-Aug. 1971   Served in Royal Air Force as flight lieutenant. Trained to Wing Standard at RAF College, Cranwell
Sept-Oct. 1971   Joined Royal Navy as acting sub-lieutenant. Six-week graduate course at Britannia Royal Naval College, Dartmouth
Nov. 1971-July 1972   Served with HMS *Norfolk*, guided missile destroyer, with rank of sub-lieutenant
July 1972 on   Shore courses in the Portsmouth area—accommodated in HMS *Dryad*—followed by familiarization flying with the Royal Navy and the Queen's Flight

Nov. 1972 on   Served with HMS *Glasserton*, coastal mine-sweeper, while waiting to join HMS *Minerva*

March-Sept. 1973   Served with HMS *Minerva,* a *Leander*-class frigate. Visited the Caribbean, South America, the United States and Canada. Gained his bridge watch-keeping certificate and ocean navigation certificate. Promoted lieutenant

April-May 1973   Served briefly with HMS *Fox,* survey ship, while *Minerva* visiting Bermuda

Oct. 1973 on   Completed shore courses for destroyer navigating officers, divisional officers and flight deck officer

Jan-Aug. 1974   Served with HMS *Jupiter,* another *Leander*-class frigate, a a watch-keeping officer

Sept-Dec. 1974   Helicopter conversion course at Royal Naval Air Station Yeovilton

Jan. 1975   Advanced flying training at Yeovilton prior to joining 845 Naval Air Squadron

March-June 1975   Served with 845 Squadron aboard HMS *Hermes,* commando ship

Sept.-Dec. 1975   Lieutenants' course (duties of a junior staff officer) at the Royal Naval College, Greenwich

Feb.-Dec. 1976   Commanded HMS *Bronington,* a minehunter of the *Ton* class, forming part of the 1st Mine Countermeasures Squadron based at Rosyth

APPENDIX VI

Witty Ditty

Sung to the hymn tune *Immortal, Invisible, God Only Wise,* the witty ditty penned by Prince Charles during his visit to Canada's Northwest Territory went something like this...

Impossible, unapproachable, God only
knows,
The light's always dreadful and he won't
damn-well pose,
Most maddening, most curious, he
simply can't fail,
It's always the same with the old Prince
of Wales.

Insistent, persistent, the press never end,
One day they will drive me right round
                                    the bend,
Recording, rephrasing, every word that I
                                        say,
It's got to be news at the end of the day.

Disgraceful, most dangerous, to share
                            the same plane,
Denies me the chance to scratch and
                                complain,
Oh where may I ask is the Monarchy
                                    going,
When princes and pressmen are on the
                            same Boeing?

The programme so formal and highly
                                arranged,
But haven't you heard that it's all been
                                changed,
Friday is Sunday and that is quite plain,
So no one, please no one, is allowed to
                                complain.